CHARTWELL

Kent

THE NATIONAL TRUST

The National Trust owes a continuing debt of gratitude to the late Lady Churchill. As Robin Fedden wrote in the first guidebook to Chartwell, 'But for her generosity and public spirit the house would have come to the Trust as an empty shell. She not only ensured that most of the contents, things with which she had lived for many years and to which she was deeply attached, should be acquired by the Treasury in payment of death duty for retention at Chartwell, but she gave many of her own possessions so that the character of the house might remain unchanged.' Many of the objects on show are loaned through the generosity of the Churchill family.

My principal debt is to Lady Soames, whose biography of her mother offers the best recent account of life at Chartwell. Lady Soames has written the Introduction and Chapter Seven for this new guidebook, and given invaluable advice on the rest. The past and present Chartwell administrators, Grace Hamblin and Jean Broome, have also put me right on numerous points; their combined knowledge of Chartwell now spans 60 years. James Bettley showed me his files on Philip Tilden and lent photographs. The Trustees of the Chartwell Trust gave me permission to consult the voluminous Chartwell estate papers in the Churchill Archive Centre, Churchill College, Cambridge. I am very grateful to the Centre's Librarian, Correlli Barnett, and Archivist, Alan Kucia, for their help. I would also like to thank the following, who have assisted me in various ways: Peregrine Bryant, Mrs E. Buxton, Mrs Winston Churchill, Arabella Churchill-Macleod, Dr John House, Ian Montrose, Anthea Morton-Saner. For permission to quote from copyright material I am grateful to the following: Macmillan Publishers (Harold Macmillan, *Winds of Change*, 1966; *Tides of Fortune*, 1969); Viscount Norwich (Diana Cooper, *The Light of Common Day*, 1959); Secker & Warburg (Piers Brendon, *Winston Churchill: A Brief Life*, 1984).

Oliver Garnett

Photographs: Broadwater Collection, Churchill College, Cambridge pages 24, 73; Mrs E. Buxton pages 14, 15; Curtis Brown Group Ltd, London, © The Churchill Heritage pages 34, 40, 41, 42, 43, 44, 48, 53; Hulton-Deutsch Collection pages 4, 22 (top and bottom), 38; Magnum/Philippe Halsman front cover; National Trust pages 13, 39, 45; National Trust Photographic Library/Don Carr page 68; NTPL/Andreas von Einsiedel pages 1, 25, 30, 37, 49, 51, 52, 54, 55, 57, 60, 63, 64, 75 (top), back cover; NTPL/Ian Shaw pages 23, 33, 67, 70, 71, 72 (top and bottom); NTPL/Rupert Truman pages 6, 12, 17, 18; NTPL/Derrick E. Witty pages 7, 8, 9, 10, 20, 21, 26 (© Elizabeth Banks), 27, 29, 31, 32, 50, 65, 75 (bottom).

First published in Great Britain in 1992 by the National Trust
© 1992 The National Trust Chapters 1–6, 8–9
© 1992 Mary Soames Introduction, Chapter 7
ISBN 0 7078 0147 8

Designed by James Shurmer
Phototypeset in Monotype Lasercomp Bembo Series 270
by Southern Positives and Negatives (SPAN), Lingfield, Surrey (8508)
Printed in Italy by Amilcare Pizzi s.p.a.
for National Trust Enterprises, 36 Queen Anne's Gate, London SW1H 9AS
Registered charity no. 205846

CONTENTS

Churchill at work on the extension to Orchard Cottage in 1939

INTRODUCTION

by Mary Soames

Chartwell was Winston and Clementine Churchill's home for 40 years. My father bought it in September 1922, in the week that I, their last child, was born, and until I was 17 it was to be my whole world.

While Winston and his children – Diana, Randolph and Sarah (and later myself) – loved Chartwell unconditionally, Clementine from the first had serious practical reservations about the whole project. Her prudent Scottish side judged the renovations (involving largely rebuilding the house), and the subsequent cost of running the whole property, would place a near intolerable strain on the Churchills' somewhat fragile financial raft. She was to be proved right, and over the years her pleasure in the place was seldom unalloyed by anxiety. Clementine, however, never stinted thought or effort in making Chartwell a delightful, comfortable home for her family, and the charming place so many friends through the years would recall. My mother imprinted the stamp of her lovely, and always unaffected, taste on both house and garden.

Winston had been captivated by Chartwell from the moment he set eyes on the valley, protected by the sheltering arm of the beautiful beech woods (sadly devastated in the 1987 gales), and by the house set on the hillside, commanding sweeping views over the Weald of Kent. The Chart Well, which rises at the top of the property, nourished the existing lake, and Winston saw at once the possibilities it provided for yet another lake, dams, swimming pools and water gardens. In all of these projects over the ensuing years, he himself would play the role of creator and artisan.

The walls enclosing the vegetable garden (built very largely with his own hands), and the dear little cottage he made for me, bear witness to his skill and assiduity as a bricklayer. Chartwell also provided countless scenes – still lifes and interiors – for

Winston's brush. The Studio at the bottom of the orchard was the place (apart from his Study) where he spent the greater number of 'indoor' hours.

But if Chartwell was his playground, it was also his 'factory'. Throughout the twenties and thirties, in or out of office, Winston Churchill was immersed in politics. The lights in the beamed Study upstairs gleamed late through the night and into the small hours, as, padding up and down the long room, he dictated for hours on end to his secretary the ceaseless stream of speeches and newspaper articles through which he waged his political campaigns. Likewise there flowed from his pen the continuous procession of books which kept his family nourished, and Chartwell from foundering.

Chartwell house parties (never very large by prevailing standards) were composed mainly of close relations and one or two cronies. But since Chartwell is only an hour's drive from London there was also a constant to-ing and fro-ing of day guests, who provided a varied and vivid company: politicians, journalists and writers, painters, and – adding a youthful zest – the elder children's friends.

During the first year of the war, Winston and Clementine spent a few weekends at Chartwell: the 'big house' was not staffed, and had its quota of evacuees. So my parents used 'Orchard Cottage' (another 'Winston' construction), situated close to the Studio. But soon Chartwell was deemed unsafe (too conspicuous from the air) and the house was dustsheeted and shut up for the duration of the war, although Winston made one or two day visits to his beloved domain. Once I went with him: we roamed the gardens, now a wilderness; the grass in the orchard was waist-high, and brambles mingled with rambler roses. From its hilltop the house gazed blindly out of shuttered windows over the desolate gardens, but there was a kind of tousled loveliness about the place.

The entrance front

Immediately after the war Clementine drastically reorganised the manner in which we inhabited Chartwell, so that only a few servants were required, in contrast to the indoor staff of eight to nine needed before the war. Gradually life and enjoyment took up again, although never on the pre-war scale. In 1946 a group of Winston's friends and admirers bought Chartwell and presented it to the National Trust, with the proviso that Winston and Clementine should live there for their lifetimes. With the future of Chartwell thus assured, and with the rosier state of Winston's finances (for which his war memoirs were largely responsible), Clementine took a new pleasure in running Chartwell and in the life there. She found it less burdensome, and she was particularly enthusiastic about garden plans, which now were not only affordable, but seemed worthwhile, as Chartwell was to be preserved for ever.

As the toll of the years mounted, Winston still found infinite pleasure and contentment at Chartwell. Grandchildren as well as children came to be company for both my parents. My mother now played croquet instead of tennis; my father would watch the butterflies hovering on the buddleias and count the red admirals with satisfaction; or sit for hours gazing out over the dim blueness of the Weald – the view that 40 years before had so enraptured him.

After Winston's death in 1965, Clementine did not wish to continue living at Chartwell, and so relinquished it to the National Trust. It was her wish that the principal rooms should be shown as much as possible as they were in Chartwell's heyday – the twenties and thirties. Accordingly, rooms which since the war had been used for different purposes, were restored to their original use. Clementine gave in perpetuity to the National Trust many pieces of furniture, carpets and *objets d'art* that had always been part of Chartwell; she also bequeathed to the Trust a collection of about 60 of Winston's own paintings for the house and Studio.

In the twelve years she lived after my father's death, my mother took a continuing and active interest in Chartwell. Right up to the summer before her death in December 1977, aged 92, she made several visits every year. It gave her great pleasure and satisfaction to see how many people thronged to Chartwell, and how they seemed to enjoy the house and gardens where Winston and she had made their home for 40 momentous years.

CHAPTER ONE
THE ROAD TO CHARTWELL

In mid-September 1922 Churchill took his three eldest children, Diana (then 13), Randolph (11) and Sarah (7), on an expedition. Sarah Churchill has described the day:

We clambered into an old Wolseley and with my father at the wheel off we went. He told us on the way down that the purpose of this journey was to inspect a house that he thought of buying in Kent, and he wanted our opinion. We were thrilled. We must have taken a picnic lunch, but this I don't remember; only the excitement of his showing us Chartwell for the first time.

Chartwell was wildly overgrown and untidy, and contained all the mystery of houses that had not been lived in for many years. We did a complete tour of the house and grounds, my father asking anxiously – it is clear in my mind – 'Do you like it?' Did we like it? We were delirious. 'Oh, do buy it! Do buy it!' we exclaimed. 'Well, I'm not sure . . .'[1]

Only when they were back in London did Churchill finally reveal that the house was already theirs. Why had Churchill decided to buy Chartwell? To understand the reasons and the kind of home it became, we must go back to the beginning.

Winston Leonard Spencer Churchill was born at 1.30am on 30 November 1874 at Blenheim Palace in Oxfordshire, the home of his grandfather, the

Blenheim Palace in Oxfordshire, the home of the Dukes of Marlborough and the birthplace, in 1874, of Winston Churchill; by an unknown English artist, 1770s (Study)

7th Duke of Marlborough, and by some way the grandest country house in England. With an impatience typical of his later life he had arrived several weeks early. Blenheim may never have been Churchill's home, for the estate and family title passed to his cousin, the 9th Duke (a lifelong friend always known as 'Sunny'), but for five years in the 1890s Churchill was heir presumptive to the dukedom, and it was always where his roots lay.

Blenheim had been created in the early eighteenth century by John Vanbrugh for Churchill's hero, the 1st and greatest Duke of Marlborough, John Churchill. Its vast baroque façades and courtyards were for Churchill tangible proof of the grandeur of Britain's history and her continuing greatness as a nation. He spent some of the happiest periods of his lonely childhood at Blenheim. In April 1882, aged seven, he wrote to his mother, 'It is so nice being in the country. The gardens and the

Churchill as a boy; pencil drawing by John Tenniel (Lady Churchill's Bedroom)

park are so much nicer to walk in than the Green Park or Hyde Park.'[2] Throughout the rest of his life Churchill returned frequently to Blenheim, most often for Christmas house parties with the Marlboroughs. In the little Temple of Diana in the gardens he proposed to his future wife in 1908. And it was within sight of Blenheim, in Bladon churchyard, that he finally chose to be buried. It is no surprise, therefore, that Churchill should have installed a view of Blenheim in the place of honour above the fireplace of his Study at Chartwell.

In the late nineteenth century, the great country houses of England such as Blenheim were still the 'power houses' of the British Empire, from which political authority was dispensed over a quarter of the planet. For most of Churchill's childhood and early manhood, the Prime Minister was the Tory Lord Salisbury, whose family home, Hatfield House in Hertfordshire, had been built by an earlier first minister, Robert Cecil. The weekend parties that Salisbury hosted at Hatfield were not only lavish social occasions, but often the setting for political high drama. At one such house party shortly before Christmas 1886, Salisbury received final confirmation that Churchill's father, Lord Randolph Churchill, had resigned after only six months as Chancellor of the Exchequer in his Conservative government. Salisbury is said to have been dining with Lord Randolph's mother, the Duchess of Marlborough, when the message arrived, and to have moved on to the next course without the flicker of an eyebrow.[3]

Resignation brought Lord Randolph's ministerial career to an end, and he died nine years later an isolated and broken man. Churchill dedicated his life to restoring his father's reputation and grasping the 'glittering prizes' that had eluded him. After hair-raising adventures on the North-West Frontier, in North Africa and the Boer War, which proved both his skill as a journalist and his physical courage under fire, Churchill entered Parliament in 1900 as Tory MP for Oldham. In his maiden speech he paid graceful tribute to his father's memory and at the same time established himself as a politician to be reckoned with. His mother, the vivacious American heiress Jennie Jerome, was watching from the Strangers' Gallery and she used all her consider-

Churchill's father, Lord Randolph Churchill, at his desk; by Edwin Ward (Study)

able charm and influence in the salons of Edwardian England to further his political career. Churchill took up with Salisbury's son, Lord Hugh Cecil, and his circle, known as the 'Hughligans', and set about honing his powers of argument on any willing audience with an almost barbaric glee. One guest at a Christmas house party remembered 'Winston making a political speech which lasted without intermission for 8 days. He was the autocrat – not only of the breakfast table – but of the lunch, tea, dinner, bridge and billiard tables.'[4] At the palatial country homes of rich friends like 'Bendor', Duke of Westminster, Churchill could also indulge his fondness for the high life and for country pursuits.

Having switched allegiances to the Liberal party, in 1908 Churchill entered Asquith's Cabinet as President of the Board of Trade, but more importantly he married. His bride was the granddaughter of the 10th Earl of Airlie, Clementine Hozier – always 'Clemmie' to Churchill and 'Kat' in their affectionate letters to one another. Her parents' marriage had not been happy, and when they separated, she had endured hard times. As a result she could never understand Churchill's cheerful extravagance, and worries over money were always to colour her feelings about Chartwell. At 23 she possessed beauty,

intelligence and fiercely independent views in a combination Churchill found entrancing. He concluded his memoir, *My Early Life*, 'I married and lived happily ever afterwards'.[5] Life, alas, is never quite that simple. Rows were inevitable between two such strong-minded people, but they never lasted long and their mutual devotion was never in doubt. Clementine fought like a tigress to defend her husband through innumerable political crises, and together they made a formidable partnership.

They set up home together in Eccleston Square, near Victoria station, while Churchill's ministerial career took him from the Board of Trade to the Home Office, and then the Admiralty. Relaxation in the country was provided by friends such as F. E. Smith and Wilfrid Scawen Blunt. They hunted and later dined with Blunt, arrayed in the gorgeous robes he had brought back from the Middle East, and talking politics all the while.[6] Such country parties could bring other excitements. While Churchill was staying at Burley-on-the-Hill in Rutland with his cousin, Freddie Guest, the house caught fire. Churchill, still in his pyjamas, tackled the blaze with fearless relish: 'Every window spouted fire & from the centre of the house a volcano roared skyward in a whirlwind of sparks'.[7]

9

Six years later a far vaster conflagration, the First World War, overwhelmed Europe, almost destroying Churchill's career and ending for ever the aristocratic certainties of the world in which he had been brought up. The disastrous outcome of the Dardanelles campaign against Turkey, of which Churchill had been the chief advocate, forced him to resign from the Admiralty in 1915. Preferring action on the Western Front to a sinecure in the tottering Asquith government, Churchill was appointed colonel of the 6th Battalion, Royal Scots Fusiliers. In the trenches he again demonstrated his courage and powers of leadership.

Churchill returned to London in May 1916 to urge the more rigorous prosecution of the war on a wider stage, becoming Minister of Munitions in Lloyd George's new Coalition government. Politics did not, however, consume all his thoughts. By 1917 the Churchills had three young children, and they were keen to find what Clementine called 'a little country basket', in which they could relax as a family away from the ceaseless demands of White-

Churchill in his uniform as colonel of the 6th Battalion, the Royal Scots Fusiliers. He is shown wearing the French infantryman's helmet that hangs below the portrait; by Sir John Lavery, 1916 (Stairs)

hall and the war.[8] In the spring of that year Churchill bought a grey stone Elizabethan manor house near East Grinstead in Sussex. Lullenden was in many ways a dress rehearsal for Chartwell. The large high-ceilinged room on the ground floor became a nursery for the children where they could play safe from the threat of air raids. The wooded grounds enclosed a lake beside which Churchill could satisfy his growing passion for painting. But although Clementine had always wanted to live in the country, she was worried about the expense of running two houses. So in September 1919 Churchill sold Lullenden to his friend, General Sir Ian Hamilton. But the seed had been sown.

Lloyd George was determined to maintain the wartime coalition of Liberal and Conservatives into peacetime, a position that was triumphantly vindicated at the 1918 election. Churchill became Secretary of State for War and Air in the new government, responsible for the huge task of demobilisation, and subsequently Colonial Secretary. On the surface the routine of pre-war social life returned – political dinner parties in London and country house weekends – but the landscape had subtly shifted. It was no longer assumed that leading politicians like Churchill would have their own country estates. A symbolic turning point was reached in 1917, when Sir Arthur Lee offered Chequers in Buckinghamshire to the nation as a country home for the Prime Minister.[9] The illusion of landed status was thereby maintained, but the reality was that, for an increasing proportion of the ever-broadening political class, the countryside was no longer the source of power, but a pleasant place to retreat to for the weekend after a busy week in Westminster. When the Lloyd George government collapsed in 1922, few were surprised that the King should pass over Lord Curzon, the master of Kedleston Hall and large estates, and turn to a landless Glasgow lawyer, Andrew Bonar Law, for a new Prime Minister.

The early 1920s were a period of sadness and turmoil in Churchill's personal and political life. His mother died in June 1921, followed three months later by the Churchills' youngest child, Marigold, at the age of only three. In the midst of the government's death throes the following autumn, Chur-

chill collapsed with acute appendicitis and was still in hospital when a general election was called in November. Clementine heroically shouldered the burden of defending his Dundee seat alone, although still nursing their last child, Mary, who was only seven weeks old. Despite her efforts Churchill and the Liberal party were soundly defeated. The Liberals, irreconcilably divided into Lloyd George and Asquith factions, were never again to form a government, and Churchill at the age of 47 seemed to be facing a similarly bleak future. He summed up his predicament with the famous words: 'In the twinkling of an eye, I found myself without an office, without a seat, without a party and without an appendix'.[10] Such public bravado concealed private despair: this was the only occasion on which his personal detective, Sergeant Thompson, ever saw him utterly dejected. Yet in the midst of disaster there was one bright note. On 11 November 1922 Churchill completed the purchase of Chartwell Manor in Kent.

NOTES

1 Sarah Churchill, *Thread in the Tapestry*, 1967, p.22.

2 WSC/Lady Randolph Churchill, April 1882. Quoted Gilbert, 1991, p.2.

3 David Cecil, *The Cecils of Hatfield House*, Constable, 1973, p.245.

4 See Brendon, p.42.

5 WSC, *My Early Life*, 1930, p.385.

6 Blunt, 1920, II, p.414.

7 Quoted Gilbert, 1991, p.197.

8 CC/WSC, 16 February 1916. Churchill papers. Quoted Soames, 1979, p.185.

9 See Mark Girouard, *Life in the English Country House*, Yale, 1978, pp.302 and 316 for these points.

10 WSC, 'Election Memories', *Thoughts and Adventures*, 1932, p.213.

CHAPTER TWO

TRANSFORMING CHARTWELL

Churchill first saw Chartwell in July 1921, when it was offered for sale with 800 acres. The setting captivated him immediately: a shallow valley enclosed to the west by Crockham Hill, to the east by Toys Hill, both clothed in ancient beech trees. In the lap of the valley was a modest lake fed by the Chart Well, from which the house set into the western hillside took its name. But most important to Churchill was the panoramic view south over the gentle landscape of the Weald of Kent towards Hever Castle. Churchill's beloved nanny, Mrs Everest, had filled his head with stories of the 'Garden of England'. The great storm of October

1987 stripped the trees from the surrounding slopes, but that view has survived remarkably unchanged by nature or the modern world. On a misty morning it still speaks powerfully of an older England of Nanny Everest's remembering. Churchill often said he had bought Chartwell for the view.

Chartwell's historical associations must also have appealed. For Henry VIII is said to have slept in an oak-panelled room (now gone) in the house, while courting Anne Boleyn at Hever Castle.[1] More prosaically, Chartwell was only 25 miles from Westminster, and could be reached by lunch guests from town in less than a hour by car.

In early 1921 Churchill still faced the money problems which had obliged him to sell Lullenden in 1919, and so he could not raise the £6,500 reserve price put on the estate. However, the idea was set aside only temporarily. Late that same year his financial position was transformed, when he inherited from a distant cousin the Garron Tower estate in County Antrim, which brought him £4,000 a year in rents and revenues. His literary earnings were also beginning to grow rapidly. By the end of 1921 he had advances totalling £22,000 from British and US publishers for the first volume of *The World Crisis*, his history of the First World War, which appeared in 1923. He estimated that he was being paid at the generous rate of half a crown a word. So when he heard in the autumn of 1922 that Chartwell and the surrounding 80 acres were still on the market, he eagerly snapped them up for £5,000. Churchill was amused to discover that the vendor, A. J. Campbell Colquhoun, had been a contemporary at Harrow, with whom he had competed for bottom place in the 4th form.[2]

Clementine's first impressions of Chartwell were as favourable as those of her husband. Pleasure soon turned to appalled dismay when she looked more closely at what they had taken on. The building itself was, to her view, irredeemably ugly. A house of some form has stood on this site since at least the sixteenth century, when the estate, known as Well Street, belonged to the Potter family.[3] In the seventeenth and eighteenth centuries the property seems not to have been the primary residence of its owners, for it changed hands with bewildering regularity, and we know virtually nothing of what was done to it. Whatever modest charm the original farmhouse may have had, was comprehensively blotted out when it was enlarged and remodelled by the Campbell Colquhoun family in the mid-nineteenth century. The result was Victorian architecture at its least attractive, a ponderous red-brick country mansion of tile-hung gables and poky oriel windows. With curious perversity the unknown architect had also turned the principal front away from the magical view and toward the nearby main road. By 1922 the hillside beyond was overrun by purple *Rhododendron ponticum*, which Clementine thought particularly hideous. The creeper that smothered the house only increased the gloom.

(Right) The garden front of Chartwell in the late nineteenth century, when it was the home of the Campbell Colquhoun family

(Left) Churchill bought Chartwell for this view

Clementine realised that Chartwell would be expensive to make habitable. The isolation of the house and the lack of nearby public transport would also make it difficult to recruit and keep servants. However, once Churchill had settled on a course of action, it was almost impossible to change his mind. He was as besotted about Chartwell as Mr Toad with a new enthusiasm, and he remained deaf to all his wife's objections. In September 1923 he tried to set her mind at rest:

My beloved, I do beg you not to worry about money, or to feel insecure. On the contrary the policy we are pursuing aims above all at *stability*. (Like Bonar Law!) Chartwell is to be our *home*. It will have cost us £20,000 and will be worth at least £15,000 apart from a fancy price. We must endeavour to live there for many years & hand it on to Randolph afterwards. We must make it in every way charming & as far as possible economically self contained. It will be cheaper than in London.[4]

Clementine was to put her own very individual stamp upon Chartwell, but she could never love it. For she felt that she should have been consulted about the decision to buy the house, and the task of keeping such a substantial establishment running through good times and bad was to be a constant burden in the 1920s and '30s. By contrast Chartwell brought Churchill 40 years of unalloyed pleasure.

Churchill chose as his architect Philip Tilden, who had made his reputation converting old, but impractical, country houses for the modern needs of a small circle of rich clients. Tilden depended for much of his work on personal recommendation, and it was probably Churchill's aunt, Lady Leslie, a friend of Tilden, who first suggested him.[5] Chur-

Philip Tilden rebuilt Chartwell for Churchill between 1922 and 1924. He is sitting in the hall of Wardes, also in Kent, which he redesigned for Sir Louis Mallet in 1917–18

Views of Chartwell during Tilden's rebuilding work: the garden front, before (bottom left) and after (top left); the entrance front, before (top middle and right) and after (bottom middle and right)

chill was a frequent visitor at Sir Philip Sassoon's house near the Kent coast, Port Lympne, where Tilden had installed a Neo-classical swimming pool. It must also have appealed to Churchill that Tilden was at the time building a completely new house, Bron-y-de, at Churt in Surrey, for Lloyd George, one of the few politicians of the era to whom he willingly deferred. Tilden saw the drawbacks of Chartwell as clearly as Clementine. On his first visit he found 'a dreary house perched on the edge of the hillside, very close to the road, but banked on its western side by a cascade of full-grown rhododendrons. So embowering were the giant trees, so encroaching was the verdure, that the red bricks of the house were slimed with green, and upon investigation I was to find that only that portion that was the kernel of the old manor, floored and raftered in old oak, had withstood the ravages of wet; the rest was weary of its own ugliness so that the walls ran with moisture and creeping fungus tracked down the cracks and crevices.'[6] But he also saw the possibilities and eagerly took on the commission.

Churchill approached the task of transforming Chartwell like an eighteenth-century patron rather than a modern client. He demanded a scale model of the kind that Vanbrugh had constructed of Blenheim for the 1st Duke. Only with considerable difficulty did Tilden convince him that perspective drawings and plans would be an acceptable substitute. When a month had passed and the designs had not appeared, Churchill began to press. Tilden was soon pleading for patience: 'it takes a very considerable amount of time and thought to produce things that matter so much'.[7] When the plans were finally delivered, Churchill was delighted with his proposals.

Tilden had two principal aims: to simplify and modernise the layout of the house, and to make the most of the valley setting. Once the ivy had been stripped off the walls and the dense surrounding shrubs removed, he began work at the south end. This he gave a stepped gable, and replanned as a separate block containing nurseries for the children, with its own staircase leading down to a kitchenette on the ground floor. In the mid-1930s Churchill converted the first floor of this block into his bedroom, the large bay window providing a splendid view over the Weald to the south.[8] Tilden, however, was entirely responsible for Churchill's adjoining first-floor Study, in which the ceiling was opened up to reveal the old roof timbers above, creating an effect of age and spaciousness reminiscent of Lullenden. French windows from the sitting-room below the Study led out on to a terrace with another fine view of the Weald.

Tilden radically simplified the west, entrance front by removing the central gabled bay. He marked the front door with an eighteenth-century doorcase of ornately carved wood, bought from the London dealers in such antique fittings, Thomas Crowther, for £25.[9] The idea of using an old wooden doorcase seems to have been Churchill's, for he wrote to Tilden in October 1923: 'There is a very striking oak door in No.– South Grosvenor Road, a home belonging to the Duke of Westminster, which is certainly very suggestive and capable of adaptation.'[10] Crowther's also supplied the ship weathervane that is the principal ornament of the roof (£20), and many of the panelled doors and cast-iron firebacks in the house. A measure of privacy from the main road was provided by a new wall enclosing the drive to the west of the house.

To create more rooms overlooking the garden and the valley beyond, Tilden constructed a completely new wing extending eastwards at right angles from the centre of the old house. Churchill proudly called this 'my promontory'. As originally planned, it would have been 12 feet longer, with an additional bedroom and dressing-room for Churchill, but even as built, it still contains three of the largest and most attractive rooms in the house.[12]

On the top floor was a barrel-vaulted bedroom for Clementine; below was the long Drawing Room; and below that the Dining Room, a full storey lower than the ground floor on the west front because of the steeply sloping site. The adjacent staircase block connected these floors.

Churchill had a painter's love of sunlight and wanted the windows throughout to be as large as possible. Tilden was insistent that the existing brick mullions and transoms should be retained, but to allow the maximum daylight in, new casements were inserted with thin metal glazing bars. The north end of the house was principally given over to the estate office and the low Kitchen wing. Tilden believed that 'the ideal house should be one which allows its domestic quarters to be alongside the dining room, well away from the rest of the house. And that is what was evolved at Chartwell.'[13] A new Kitchen and Pantry (painted blue to ward off flies) were built on the same lower ground-floor level as the Dining Room, with such modern conveniences as a built-in electric hotplate to keep food warm.[14] Water was piped in by the local water company, supplemented by a hydraulic ram on the property. It was needed in substantial quantities, for Shanks & Co. supplied no fewer than 5 baths and 14 lavatories.[15] Churchill also had telephones installed to keep him in touch with events in London.

Many years later Tilden concluded somewhat ruefully, 'No client that I have ever had, considering his well-filled life, has ever spent more time, trouble, or interest in the making of his home than did Mr Churchill.' The Churchills paid frequent visits in late 1922 to discuss the house with Tilden over working picnics. In the summer of 1923 the whole family stayed at Hosey Rigge, a house near Westerham, to oversee operations. (The children promptly renamed it 'the Rosy Pig'.)[16] Nothing escaped Churchill's eye for detail, from the best shape for light switches (square) to the capacity of the overflow pipes. From the start there were problems. The dryrot proved difficult to eradicate, water poured into the house through the new Nursery wing gable, cracks appeared in the floors and ceiling of the garden wing, chimneys smoked, chandeliers collapsed and faults were discovered in the wiring. And all the while Churchill's fertile

The elegant eighteenth-century wooden doorcase was bought by Tilden from a London antique dealer

The garden front

brain was devising improvements not envisaged in the original plans. Costs rose inexorably from the initial estimate of £7,000 to over £18,000, until Churchill and Tilden were barely on speaking terms – a sad echo of the disputes between Duchess Sarah and Vanbrugh that dogged the building of Blenheim.[17] As the building work dragged on into 1924, Churchill began to despair of seeing an end to it: 'So important to get it *finished*, and get the grass and greenery growing. "Finish" – that is the vital thing,' he wrote to Clementine.[18]

On 17 April 1924 Churchill could finally tell his wife: 'This is the first letter I have ever written from this place, & it is right that it shd be to you. I am in bed in your bedroom (wh I have annexed temporarily) & wh is sparsely but comfortably furnished with the pick of yr two van loads.'[19] The house that Tilden created may not have been particularly striking, but it suited Churchill admirably. In November 1924 he predicted, 'Chartwell, in spite of the difficulties and expenses which have attended its construction, will be looked upon as a very graceful and pleasant country house.'[20] He never had any reason to change his opinion.

The large, airy interiors of the new Chartwell very quickly took on the personalities of the Churchills. Clementine decorated the house in contemporary 1920s style and with a simple good taste that has hardly dated. She favoured plain, light colours for the walls and ceilings: cream in most of the rooms, pale grey in the Drawing Room, duck egg blue in her bedroom. Bright colour and pattern were provided by the glazed chintz curtains: flowery in the Library and Drawing Room, a dramatic emerald green in the Dining Room.[21] The furniture was an agreeable mixture. A few old family pieces, such as the mahogany desk and bureau-bookcase in the Study, came down from London, but no more than that – Clementine rated practicality above antiquity. Comfortable new sofas and armchairs covered in pale fabrics filled the Drawing Room. She also bought modern designs, most notably the circular, scrubbed oak tables and dining chairs in the Dining Room, which were supplied by Heal's. There was even the occasional special commission, like the sideboard against the south wall of the Dining Room, designed by Tilden for the Churchills and also built by Heal's.

Churchill gave his wife a free hand in decorating the house, but occasionally intervened, for example to specify the requirements for the Dining Room chairs in characteristic detail:

The Dining Room chair has certain very marked requisites. First, it should be comfortable and give support to the body when sitting up straight: it should certainly have arms, which are an enormous comfort when sitting at meals. Second, it should be compact. One does not want the Dining Room chair spreading itself, or its legs, or its arms, as if it were a plant, but an essentially upright structure with the arms and the back almost perpendicularly over the legs. This enables the chairs to be put together if need be, which is often more sociable, while at the same time the arms prevent undue crowding and elbowing.[22]

In April 1924 A. Luff & Sons, Landscape Gardeners and Nurserymen, offered their services to Churchill. But just as Clementine would not have dreamt of employing a professional interior decorator, so Churchill determined to remake the extensive gardens himself and in his own way. The ground slopes away quite sharply from the east side of the house towards the bottom of the valley, and so the first task was to build up a broad grassy terrace next to the house behind a brick embankment. Tilden designed an elegant summer-house to stand on one corner of this terrace, which was decorated in 1949 by Churchill's nephew, John Spencer Churchill, with murals and *trompe-l'oeil* plaques celebrating the Marlborough wars. The idea of the Marlborough Pavilion, as it is now known, seems to have been Clementine's, for Churchill himself told Tilden:

There is too much made of the romance and usefulness of garden houses, for not only, as you sit there, do spiders, suspended by their invisible threads, alight upon your head, but your feet are not immune from the constant attack of those little woodlice, that career, like so many tanks, across the floor; not to speak of insects too numerous to mention, that seem to like one's tea even more than one does oneself.[23]

Churchill next turned his attention to the lake at the bottom of the valley. For someone brought up to admire Capability Brown's lakes at Blenheim, it must have seemed altogether too modest, and he spent most of the summers of 1924 and 1925 expanding it. He was never happier than when at work on such projects, 'wallowing in the most filthy black mud you ever saw, with the vilest odour'.[24] In September 1925 he wrote to Stanley Baldwin, 'The days have slipped away very quickly here. I have passed them almost entirely in the open air, making a dam, which largely extends my lake and finally, I hope, removes it from the category of ponds.'[25] The lake remained a happy obsession, with which he continued to tinker throughout the 1930s. In the Chartwell garden at least, Churchill was his own master, and into it he was to throw all the frustrated energy of a politician out of power.

NOTES

1 Thomas Jones diary, 25 August 1926. Jones papers. Quoted Gilbert, *Companion*, V, i, 1979, p.746.

2 A.J. Campbell Colquhoun/WSC, 25 September 1922. Churchill papers 1/159.

3 Hasted, III, 1797, p.168.

4 WSC/CC, 2 September 1923. Spencer-Churchill papers. Quoted Gilbert, *Companion*, V, i, 1979, p.58.

5 Tilden, 1954, pp.49–50.

6 Ibid., p.116.

7 PT/WSC, 3 October 1922. Churchill papers 1/159.

8 See PT/WSC, 17 January 1923. Churchill papers 1/167.

9 Undated bill. Churchill papers 1/395.

10 WSC/PT, 29 October 1923. Churchill papers 1/395.

11 WSC memo, n.d. [1924]. Churchill papers 1/395.

12 PT/WSC, 17 January 1923. Churchill papers 1/167.

13 Tilden, 1954, p.117.

14 PT/Brown, 27 March 1924. Churchill papers 1/173.

15 Shanks bill, 12 July 1923. Churchill papers 1/167.

16 Soames, 1979, p.222.

17 WSC memo, n.d. [1924]. Churchill papers 1/395.

18 WSC/CC, 17 February 1924. Spencer-Churchill papers. Quoted Gilbert, *Companion*, V, i, 1979, p.106.

19 WSC/CC, 17 April 1924. Spencer-Churchill papers. Quoted Gilbert, *Companion*, V, i, 1979, p.144.

20 WSC/Brown, 25 November 1924. Churchill papers 1/173.

21 Soames, 1979, p.224.

22 WSC memo, n.d. Churchill papers 1/157.

23 Tilden, 1954, p.119.

24 WSC/CC, 19 August 1924. Spencer-Churchill papers. Quoted Gilbert, *Companion*, V, i, 1979, p.178.

25 WSC/Baldwin, 7 September 1925. Churchill papers 18/11. Quoted Gilbert, *Companion*, V, i, 1979, p.542.

CHAPTER THREE

LIFE AT CHARTWELL

During the two years it took Tilden to rebuild Chartwell, the political landscape of Britain changed dramatically. The long period of Liberal ascendancy was over, to be replaced by Conservative governments under Andrew Bonar Law and then Stanley Baldwin. These two years also witnessed Churchill's gradual move to the right, as he sought a new seat in Parliament. At a by-election in 1923 he still stood as a Liberal in favour of Free Trade, but was defeated. By February 1924 he had become a 'Constitutionalist' (or anti-Socialist) candidate; again he failed to be elected. He was only finally returned in October of that year as member for Epping, the constituency (later known as Wanstead and Woodford) he was to represent for the next 39 years. By this stage he was ready to rejoin the Conservative fold he had left in 1904, although he was still not officially a member of the party. It came as a considerable shock, therefore, when Baldwin offered him the post of Chancellor of the Exchequer. This was one of the rare occasions when Churchill was left speechless:

There was another pause. Then he said 'Perhaps you will now tell me what is your answer to my question. Will you go to the Treasury?' I should have liked to have answered, 'Will the bloody duck swim?' but as it was a formal and important conversation I replied, 'This fulfils my ambition. I still have my father's robe as Chancellor. I shall be proud to serve you in this splendid Office.'[1]

For the next five years Churchill threw all his energies into the job, promoting social reform, returning Britain to the gold standard in April 1925, and organising the government newspaper, *The British Gazette*, during the General Strike of May 1926. These were years of unusual contentment for Churchill, and Chartwell had much to do with this. 11 Downing Street was his official London residence, but Chartwell was home and a useful stage on which to rehearse his policies:

By imbuing the drear intricacies of economics with the glory of war Churchill gave them urgency and excitement. He held financial conferences at Chartwell, discussed fiscal measures at the dinner-table, dictated budget proposals in his bath – wallowing, gurgling, turning the taps on and off with his toes, and surfacing with a noise like a whale blowing. He strode up and down his room, his head thrust out, his thumbs stuck in the armholes of his waistcoat, conjuring up a host of dramatic strategies, illuminating them with the lights and colours of his imagination.[2]

(Left) Churchill was Chancellor of the Exchequer from 1924 (the year he moved into Chartwell) until 1929. He is wearing the ceremonial robes he had inherited from his father, who was Chancellor briefly in 1886; charcoal drawing by John Singer Sargent, 1925 (Lobby)

Politics was only one aspect of life at Chartwell in the late 1920s. Indeed it was entirely appropriate that the rebuilding should have begun with the nurseries. For Churchill had bought the house to be a family home, in which his four young children could grow up. He had worshipped his parents, but from afar, and he was determined that his own children should not lack affection. He demanded absolute quiet when he was working in the Study, but when that was over, he joined in alarmingly strenuous high-jinks with his children. Imitating a gorilla was a particular favourite. He also enjoyed charades and amateur theatricals in the Dining Room, which could easily be turned into an impromptu stage by drawing the central curtains.

The children loved the garden as much as their father, who made it a place of enchantment for them. He built his three elder children an elaborate tree-house, and his youngest, Mary, a little brick summer-house, which was christened the 'Mary-cot'. Mary, aged five, laid the foundation stone in August 1928 with Churchillian aplomb, as her father recorded:

She was presented with a bouquet . . . and then manifested a great desire to make a speech. We all had to stand for five minutes while she remained deep in thought, her lips frequently moving over the sentences. In the end she said she regarded it as a great honour to have been called upon to lay this foundation stone and that she hopes she would spend many happy hours in the house when it was finished. (Loud cheers.)[3]

Churchill also commemorated the moment in paint (Studio, south wall).

Christmas was the highlight of the family's year, when the house was decorated with ivy, laurel, yew and holly. Mary Soames recalls the scene: 'When we were all assembled on Christmas Eve, the double doors between the drawing-room and the library were flung open to reveal the Christmas tree, glowing with light, and radiating warmth, and a piny, waxy smell from a hundred real white wax candles.'[4]

An important part of the Chartwell family was the staff, who kept the house running smoothly through triumph and disaster under Clementine's watchful eye. In the pre-war years Chartwell

Diana and Sarah Churchill; by Charles Sims, 1922 (Inner Hall)

required no fewer that eight or nine indoor servants, plus a chauffeur, three gardeners, a groom for the polo ponies and an estate bailiff. Churchill could behave like a spoilt child and expected his secretaries to put in long hours, but he was in general a considerate employer, who was always enormous fun to work for. When the old gardener, Edmund Waterhouse, who had been at Chartwell over 30 years, retired in 1927, he was encouraged by Churchill to build a bungalow in Westerham, taking advantage of legislation Churchill had himself introduced as Chancellor. Much thought was given to renovating the cottage used by the chauffeur, Howes, who taught the Churchill children to drive. At the heart of Chartwell was Grace Hamblin, who arrived as a young secretary in 1932 and over the years became an indispensable support to the whole family.

Although Chartwell was used principally as a weekend home in the 1920s, Churchill harboured pretensions to be a gentleman farmer. In May 1923 he was buying pedigree Middle White pigs (sire

(Left) Churchill tiling the roof of Orchard Cottage

(Below) Churchill at his desk in the Study

One of the Australian black swans on the Chartwell lake

Rupert of Southash, dam Edenbridge Pearl), and for the first two years he kept a dairy herd. Unfortunately, neither Churchill nor his wife had the least knowledge of farming, and the demands of government hardly gave them the time to acquire it. Their animals tended either to die of disagreeable diseases or become fond pets. This letter from Churchill to his wife is typical of his softheartedness:

A minor catastrophe has occurred in the pig world. Our best new sow, irritated by the noise of a pick-axe breaking the ground near the pig sty, killed six of a new litter of eight little pigs. She was condemned to be fattened and to die, but to-day she has received the remaining two and proposes to bring them up in a sensible manner. She is therefore reprieved on probation.[5]

After 1929 Churchill had more time to contemplate the plight of his pigs. In the May election of that year the Conservative government was defeated by Ramsay MacDonald's Labour party. Churchill's brand of Edwardian oratory and fervent anti-Socialism was increasingly out of step with the mood of the times. At the age of 55 he seemed once again, and this time finally, to have reached the end of his ministerial career. The Wall Street Crash of November 1929, which wiped out most of his investments, dealt him a further blow. The house was mothballed for a time, and the family retreated to the Well Street cottage which Churchill had built at the southern end of the garden. (It was later used by the butler and is now the Administrator's house.) However, Churchill's unquenchable energy and optimism could not be held in check for long. He set about restoring the family finances with the single-mindedness of a latter-day Walter Scott. A torrent of lucrative newspaper articles and books poured from his fertile brain, bearing the address 'Chartwell, Westerham, Kent'.

When not absorbed in politics or writing, Churchill returned to the Chartwell garden. A substantial rockery and waterfall were created north-east of the house. According to a nephew, 'Monstrous lorries panted in from the depths of Wales carrying colossal chunks of mountainside.'[6] Golden orfe, supplied by Harrod's, filled nearby pools. Australian black swans and mandarin ducks (a present from Philip Sassoon) were introduced to the lake and became a frequent motif in Churchill's paintings of the garden. Despite fencing and a searchlight attached to a bicycle wheel that rotated throughout the night, there were regular losses to the local foxes. (Its modern replacement has proved more successful.) Clementine was a keen tennis player and laid out a new grass court where the vegetable garden had once been, south of the house. The choice of flowers in the garden was very much hers. She filled the formal rose garden designed by her cousin Venetia Montagu with *Lilium regale*, ceanothus, catmint and fuchsias, and trained climbing roses and clematis against the enclosing walls. Clementine also made sure that there were always fresh cut flowers in the house.

The kitchen garden beyond the tennis court was enclosed by stout red-brick walls laid by Churchill's own hand. He took justifiable pride in his skill and speed as a bricklayer: 90 bricks an hour was not uncommon. His achievements soon became public knowledge and in 1928 he took out a card as an adult apprentice in the Amalgamated Union of Building Trade Workers. Old and unsightly trees were grubbed up, and new stock planted: quinces, nut trees, pears, plums and apples, including such rare varieties as Braddick's Nonpareil and Barnack

Beauty, all came from the famous Maidstone nursery of George Bunyard.

While Clementine was away on a restorative cruise in the Pacific in the summer of 1935, Churchill turned again to work on his lake. It needed an island in the middle, he felt, and he hired a No. 4 Ruston Excavator to create one. In a series of 'Chartwell Bulletins' to Clementine, he described the misadventures of this temperamental machine, which cut a muddy swathe through the landscape and at one point sank almost inextricably into the bed of the emptied lake.

Another major project was the swimming pool, which was built in the early 1930s. Churchill had enjoyed the open-air pool at Harrow and swimming was always one of his favourite relaxations. However, he was not fond of cold water, and so had two coke-fired boilers constructed to keep the pool at a friendly 75°, even in the depths of winter. Lady Diana Cooper was at a typical Chartwell party in the 1930s:

Excavating the lakes

Forty winks in the afternoon and then (unexpectedly) bathing at 7 in pouring rain, intensely cold with a grey half-light of approaching night, yet curiously enough very enjoyable in its oddness. Freda [Dudley] Ward, Winston, Duff [Cooper], Clemmie, Randolph and a child, in fact the whole party, were splashing about with gleeful screams in this sad crepuscule. The secret is that the bath is heated, and it is Winston's delightful toy. Just now, again, twenty-four hours later, he called for Inches the butler, and said: "Tell Allen to heave a lot more coal on. I want the thing full blast." Inches returned to say that Allen was out for the day. "Then tell Arthur I want it full blast," but it was Arthur's day out as well, so the darling old schoolboy went surreptitiously and stoked himself for half an hour, coming in on the verge of apoplexy. Again we all had to bathe in the afternoon.[7]

The visitors' book on the Hall table records the names of the family, friends and political allies that were to be so much a part of life at Chartwell in the 1930s. Inevitably, as the years passed, some of Churchill's oldest companions were missing. In 1930 F. E. Smith, by then the Earl of Birkenhead, and 'the most loyal, faithful, valiant friend any man could have', died, to be followed four years later by 'Sunny' Marlborough.[8] But there were many more to take their place. Churchill's younger brother, Jack, often stayed the weekend with his family, as did Clementine's sister, Nellie, with her husband, Bertram Romilly, and their two adventurous young sons. The most frequent signature to be found in the visitors' book is that of the Oxford physicist and statistician Frederick Lindemann, always known as 'the Prof'. It would be difficult to think of anyone less like Churchill than this anti-Semitic, teetotal, vegetarian non-smoker, but he soon became one of his most trusted advisers. Lindemann had the rare gift of being able to make complex scientific ideas intelligible to the layman. Churchill once challenged him to explain the Quantum Theory in five minutes, and he did so with ease. Churchill was fascinated by the practical applications of modern science, and relied on Lindemann to keep him abreast of developments. Clementine could forgive his rather starchy manner, because he was an easy guest, but also, somewhat surprisingly, tennis champion of Sweden and so an ideal partner on the Chartwell court.

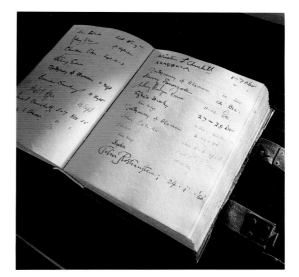

The Chartwell visitors' book

Rather less welcome, to Clementine at least, was Brendan Bracken. During the 1930s this mysterious red-haired young man with a flair for publicity was Churchill's most faithful acolyte; it was widely whispered that he was also his illegitimate son. Neither Churchill nor Bracken did much to dispel this totally baseless gossip, to Clementine's understandable annoyance. Sunday at Chartwell became known as 'Brendan day', so regular were his visits from London, when he made a lively foil for Churchill's conversational sallies over lunch.

Churchill also used Chartwell weekends to cultivate the powerful proprietors of the *Daily Express* and the *Daily Telegraph*, Lords Beaverbrook and Camrose. Another welcome guest was the American businessman Bernard Baruch, who helped to restore Churchill's finances after the 1929 Crash. Sir Edward Marsh, Churchill's former private secretary and the patron of much new art and writing, was a valued literary adviser. Less frequent, but more exciting for the children, were the times when T. E. Lawrence roared up the drive on his motorcycle and dressed for dinner in the burnous of an arabian warlord; or when Charlie Chaplin came to stay and entertained them with a little gentle slapstick.

These were some of the principal members of the

Breakfast at Chartwell. William Nicholson was a regular visitor to Chartwell in the 1930s, when he painted this unfinished scene of Winston and Clementine Churchill taking breakfast in the Dining Room. On the table is their much-loved marmalade cat, Tango

Chartwell cast in the 1930s, but at the centre of the stage was always Churchill. His daily routine changed little during these years. He woke about 7.30 and over breakfast in bed read his letters and all the national newspapers. Breakfast was usually a substantial meal, often including roast beef. He would then work, still in bed, for a couple of hours, dictating memos, letters or articles to one of his two secretaries or correcting proofs. At 11 he got up, had a bath, and, on a fine day, walked in the garden,

feeding his swans and fish. After a weak whisky and soda he returned to work in the Study. Guests often had work of their own to do, and were left to fend for themselves or be entertained by Clementine during the morning. At 1 the family and their guests gathered for lunch, which usually consisted of three expertly cooked courses. Clementine drank claret, Churchill champagne, when the family's finances would allow. Pol Roger was his preferred brand and a refrigerator given him by Lord Beaverbrook ensured that it came to table at exactly the right temperature. Generous quantities of port, brandy and cigars followed, so that if the conversation was particularly lively, the meal might not finish before 3.30.

In the afternoon Churchill would return to the

Study, or, in the summer, supervise whatever operations were underway in the garden. On winter afternoons he would enjoy a game of mah jong, and after the war bezique or backgammon, with Clementine in the Drawing Room. About 5 he would have another whisky and soda, before retiring to bed for the next hour and a half. He learnt the habit of taking a siesta while a young war correspondent in Cuba and it was to become crucial to his achievements as Prime Minister. It allowed him, he said, to pack a day and a half's work into every 24 hours. At 6.30 he would awake refreshed, take another bath and dress for dinner.

Tabletalk is notoriously difficult to convey on the page. Churchill never found his Boswell, but enough has been recorded to suggest the flavour of those evenings around the Chartwell dining-table. The political crisis of the moment might provide a starting point, on which Churchill would happily discourse in trenchant terms until one of the braver guests sought to contradict him. This would stimulate him to further rapier-like thrusts, which only the most nimble-witted could counter. From current politics conversation might leap to historical precedents, whether from Churchill's own long political career or his immense knowledge of British history. The tabletop would sometimes become a

battlefield as he re-enacted the charge of the British cavalry at the Battle of Omdurman with pepper pots and salt cellars. The 'Prof' was brought into the conversation to provide scientific reinforcement for Churchill's argument. Having committed reams of English poetry to memory, Churchill was rarely short of an apt quotation to settle his point. He needed little excuse to launch into a favourite like 'Lars Porsena of Clusium by the Nine Gods he swore . . .' Clementine tried to keep the conversation general, but it was often a vain struggle, as most guests eventually sank back in defenceless laughter before the relentless tides of Churchillian monologue. Clementine herself was happy to listen, unless someone said something particularly fatuous or offensive, when she could be roused to a sudden and crushing retort. When Churchill and his guests were well matched, conversation could continue over the cigars for many hours after the ladies had withdrawn to the Drawing Room. Often the company finally retired to bed well after midnight. Churchill, however, climbed the stairs to the Study and settled down for a further hour or more of dictation to a secretary, or telephoned the *Daily Mail* night editor for the latest news.

At Chartwell Churchill was listened to, but within the Conservative party he was becoming an

This caricature of the Other Club (founded by Churchill in 1911) suggests something of the flavour of dinners at Chartwell. Churchill appears raising pipe and glass aloft in the centre; Brendan Bracken at the extreme left, opening a bottle; Prof. Lindemann fourth from the right

increasingly isolated figure. His campaign against self-rule for India won him few friends, and in January 1931 he resigned from Baldwin's shadow cabinet. There were even fewer in Parliament willing to listen to him after 1933, when he warned that the rise of Hitler and Mussolini threatened the peace of Europe, and that Britain's defences were hopelessly ill-prepared to meet the challenge. New guests started to appear at the Chartwell dinner-table, bringing disturbing news from Whitehall. Desmond Morton, Director of the government's Industrial Intelligence Centre and a neighbour, passed on confidential assessments of the German air force's growing strength. In April 1935 Ralph Wigram, a senior official in the Foreign Office, spent the first of several weekends at Chartwell telling Churchill of his desperate concern. As Churchill later wrote of Wigram, 'He saw as clearly as I did, but with more certain information, the awful peril which was closing in upon us.'9 Churchill confronted the government in the Commons with the unanswerable statistics, but Neville Chamberlain refused to be swayed from his policy of appeasement.

Churchill's isolation and impotence seemed total. In February 1938 the news reached Chartwell that Anthony Eden, the one man in the government who had stood up to the dictators, had resigned. 'My heart sank,' Churchill wrote, 'and for a while the dark waters of despair overwhelmed me . . . From midnight till dawn I lay in my bed consumed by emotions of sorrow and fear . . . I watched the daylight slowly creep in through the windows, and saw before me in mental gaze the vision of Death.'10 The following month there was more bad news on the personal front. Churchill suddenly found himself £18,000 in debt, when the value of his US investments collapsed. There seemed no alternative but to sell Chartwell and he put the house on the market. However, Bracken came to his rescue, and with the help of a banker friend, Sir Henry Strakosch, Chartwell was saved. As the international situation worsened following the British capitulation at Munich in September 1938, Churchill's morale, perversely, improved. He had been dismissed as a sabre-rattling Cassandra, but now one by one his predictions were coming true, and he

sensed that his hour was at hand. Harold Macmillan was lunching at Chartwell in April 1939 when Mussolini invaded Albania, and has described the scene:

Maps were brought out, secretaries were marshalled; telephones began to ring. 'Where was the British fleet?' That was the most urgent question. That considerable staff which, even as a private individual, Churchill always maintained to support his tremendous outflow of literary and political effort was at once brought into play . . . I shall always have a picture of that spring day and the sense of power and energy, the great flow of action, which came from Churchill, although he then held no public office.11

Churchill spent most of the summer at Chartwell, working on his *History of the English-Speaking Peoples* and chafing at the government's inaction. 'It is a relief in times like these to be able to escape into other centuries,' he wrote to G. M. Young.12 But Churchill was not to be denied many weeks longer. At 11.15 am on Sunday, 3 September 1939 Chamberlain broadcast to the nation: '. . . I have to tell you now that no such undertaking has been received, and that consequently this country is at war with Germany.' A few hours later he summoned Churchill and offered him his old job of First Lord of the Admiralty in the new War Cabinet. The signal went round the Fleet: *Winston is back.*

NOTES

1 WSC private note. Churchill papers 4/96. Quoted Gilbert, *V. 1922–1939*, p.107.

2 Brendon, 1984, p.107.

3 WSC/CC, 10 August 1928. Spencer-Churchill papers. Quoted Gilbert, *Companion*, V, i, 1979, p.1325.

4 Soames, 1979, p.233.

5 WSC/CC, 22 October 1927. Spencer-Churchill papers. Quoted Gilbert, *Companion*, V, i, 1979, p.1065.

6 John Spencer Churchill, *Crowded Canvas*, 1961, p.59.

7 Cooper, 1959, p.155.

8 *The Times* appreciation, 30 September 1930. Quoted Gilbert, *Companion*, V, ii, 1981, p.188.

9 WSC, *The Second World War*, I, 1948, p.63.

10 Ibid., p.201.

11 Macmillan, 1966, p.592.

12 WSC/Young, 31 August 1939. Churchill papers 8/625. Quoted Gilbert, *V. 1922–1939*, 1976, p.1106.

CHAPTER FOUR

WAR

The evacuation of London had begun in August 1939. Two families from the East End were sent down to Chartwell shortly afterwards. In the alien surroundings of rural Kent they soon felt homesick and when the long-feared bombing of London failed to materialise, they returned to the capital.[1] Like many country houses, Chartwell was closed up for the war. Its location was well known, and although attempts were made to disguise Churchill's famous lakes with brushwood, it was considered vulnerable to attack by German bombers.

On 10 May 1940 Churchill was made Prime Minister. He wrote later: 'I felt as if I were walking with destiny, and that all my past life had been but a preparation of this hour and for this trial.'[2] Chequers in Buckinghamshire became Churchill's country retreat, but, like Chartwell, it was within range of the enemy, and so, 'when the moon was high' in the early weekends of the war, his considerable entourage moved to Ditchley Park, the Oxfordshire home of Ronald and Nancy Tree. In the splendid surroundings of this James Gibbs mansion Churchill re-created the pattern of country house weekends at Chartwell in the 1930s, with a siesta at 5.30, Pol Roger champagne for dinner, and brandy, cigars and conversation into the small hours.[3] One new feature of the Ditchley weekends was the evening film show, which Churchill was to copy at Chequers, and at Chartwell after the war. *Lady Hamilton*, starring Vivien Leigh as Emma and Laurence Olivier as Nelson, became a particular favourite. But the red dispatch boxes in the hall and the generals round the dinner-table underlined the daunting scale of the responsibilities he had assumed.

The war consumed Churchill's every waking hour, but his thoughts still occasionally strayed back to his beloved Chartwell, from where hampers of fruit and vegetables were sent up to No. 10 every Monday.[4] The three-bedroomed Orchard Cottage, which Churchill had been extending over the previous two years, became a welcome refuge. On 19 May 1940, as France was falling, Churchill came down to Chartwell for a few hours of sunshine and tranquillity in which to prepare the first of his famous broadcasts to the nation. That evening he spoke of 'the battle for our Island – for all that Britain is, and Britain means.'[5] In the skies above the little Chart valley the Battle of Britain was fought

(Right) Churchill in 1942, wearing one of his famous 'siren suits'; by Frank O. Salisbury (Library)

out through the summer of 1940. During air raids the gardener left in charge at Chartwell, Albert Hill, used to hide with his family in the silver safe in the 'big house' until a proper shelter was built in the grounds.[6] In June 1941, after the fall of Crete and the failure of Operation Battleaxe, Churchill returned to Chartwell. Clad in a purple dressing-gown and grey felt hat, he wandered through the gardens, showing off the goldfish to his private secretaries and at the same time ruminating on how the offensive in the Western Desert could be resumed against Rommel.[7] Finally, he decided that Wavell must be replaced as British Commander-in-Chief in the Middle East.

Churchill was at Chartwell once more in May 1942 during his anxious negotiations with Roosevelt about the convoys to Russia. His first thoughts were again for his animals. As he told Randolph: 'I went to Chartwell last week and found Spring there in all its beauty. The goose I called the naval aide-de-camp and the male black swan have both fallen victims to the fox. The Yellow Cat however made me sensible of his continuing friendship, although I had not been there for eight months.'[8] When the cat later died during one of the blackest weeks of the war, Clementine insisted that the news be kept from her husband, because she knew how much it meant to him. Churchill spent another day at Chartwell in June 1943 to check on the health of his fish, all the time dictating a stream of memos to a harassed secretary.[9] During one of the wartime conferences Churchill told Stalin how fond he was of goldfish. 'Would you like some for breakfast?' was the Soviet leader's reply.[10]

Having led Britain to total victory in Europe, Churchill was stunned by his election defeat in July 1945. Instinctively, he returned to Chartwell, to walk through the overgrown gardens with his daughter Mary and ponder on the future.[11]

NOTES

1 Soames, 1979, p.283.

2 WSC, *The Second World War*, I, 1948, p.601.

3 See Tree, 1975, especially pp.130–5.

4 Gilbert, *Companion*, V, ii, 1981, p.282.

5 Gilbert, *VI. Finest Hour, 1939–1941*, 1983, p.364.

6 Gilbert, *Companion*, V, ii, 1981, p.282.

7 Colville, 1985, p.403.

8 WSC/RC, 2 May 1942. Churchill papers 1/369. Quoted Gilbert, *VI, Finest Hour, 1939–1941*, 1983, p.99.

9 Gilbert, *VII. Road to Victory. 1941–1945*, 1986, p.433.

10 See Brendon, 1984, p.3.

11 See Pelling, 1974, p.558.

Churchill's great wartime ally, the US president Franklin Roosevelt; by Jo Davidson (Library)

CHAPTER FIVE
INDIAN SUMMER

After six years of ceaseless work and travel, both the Churchills were exhausted and Clementine hoped that her husband, now 70, would consider retirement. Might not the election defeat be a blessing in disguise? 'At the moment,' Churchill replied, 'it seems quite effectively disguised.'[1] There was also some doubt as to whether they would return to the big house at Chartwell. The children were now grown up, staff were increasingly difficult to find and such a large house would be hard to keep warm in an era of fuel rationing. They toyed with the idea of building a new, smaller home on the opposite side of the valley and turning Chartwell into a Churchill museum. However, Churchill was not yet willing to become a museum-piece. After he had spent a relaxing holiday painting and writing at Field-Marshal Alexander's villa on Lake Como, they set about opening up Chartwell. As Clementine wrote to a cousin in October 1945, 'After six years, Chartwell is liberated! It's in a sad state but we go down every weekend & struggle amid piles of dusty & mildewed books & are told by the gardener that the garden can *never* be got back!'[2] To make the house more manageable, she decided to abandon the large kitchen, scullery and pantry on the lower ground floor. The Dining Room on the same level became a cinema for weekly film shows, and a new, smaller dining-room was made out of a bedroom on the first floor, with a kitchen to serve it on the floor above. Clementine's bedroom was used as a sitting-room and later as a dining-room whilst the ground-floor sitting-room became her bedroom. Churchill kept his Study and bedroom on the first floor, but turned the Drawing Room into a studio for a while, before it reverted to its former use.

German prisoners-of-war were put to work outside removing the air-raid shelter, clearing the brushwood camouflage out of the fish pond and swimming pool, and rescuing what fish had sur-vived the depredations of the herons. The garden was tidied up and once again became a place of solace for Churchill. Here he could walk, paint to his heart's content or feed the ducks. He was anxious that modern farming methods were killing off Britain's tortoiseshell butterflies and so called in the butterfly farmer Hugh Newman for advice on how best to reintroduce them to the Chartwell garden. As a concession to stiffening limbs, the tennis court became a croquet lawn, where matches were still fought out with vigour. During the winters the house was often shut up, while the Churchills

Clementine Churchill in 1946; by Douglas Chandor (Drawing Room)

enjoyed the more friendly climate of the French Riviera.

Despite Clementine's reorganisation of the house, by 1946 the Churchills were becoming increasingly doubtful about whether they could afford to continue living at Chartwell. Their old friend Lord Camrose immediately determined to save Chartwell: a grateful nation had presented Blenheim to the 1st Duke of Marlborough; it could hardly deprive its wartime saviour of his own home. Camrose assembled a group of rich men, who together and anonymously agreed to buy Chartwell on the condition that the Churchills should be allowed to continue living there undisturbed for the rest of their lives. The house would then be presented to the National Trust as a permanent memorial to his achievements. The names of these generous benefactors are now recorded on a plaque on the garden terrace. Churchill was deeply touched, writing to Lord Camrose, 'You may be sure that Clemmie and I will do our

utmost to invest the house and gardens with every characteristic and trophy that will make it of interest in the future.'[3]

Chartwell was safe and Churchill's money worries vanished with the world-wide syndication of his multi-volume war memoirs and *History of the English-Speaking Peoples*, which made him a rich man. Numerous acts of quiet generosity to friends, family and colleagues followed. He was now able to buy Chartwell Farm and the neighbouring Parkside Farm to the south of the house, and also Bardogs Farm on Toys Hill. Until 1957, when the farms were sold, they were managed by Christopher Soames, who had married Churchill's daughter, Mary, in 1947. Soames was to prove an invaluable companion and aide to Churchill. He also entered British politics, becoming a cabinet minister in the Macmillan government, and later a notably successful British Ambassador in Paris and pioneering EEC Commissioner in Brussels. Encouraged by Christopher Soames, Churchill indulged his love of

Colonist II, the most famous horse to race in the Churchill colours; by Raoul Millais, 1951 (Drawing Room)

The Golden Rose Walk

horses by becoming a racehorse owner. From 1949 Walter Nightingall trained his horses with considerable success. The most celebrated horse in the Churchill colours was undoubtedly Colonist II, which won £13,000 in prize money in the early 1950s. When Nightingall suggested that the horse be put out to stud at the end of its career, Churchill is said to have replied, 'To stud? And have it said that the Prime Minister of Great Britain is living on the immoral earnings of a horse?'[4]

In the 1946 New Year Honours list Churchill was awarded the Order of Merit, the first of a succession of honours and gifts he was to receive from all over the world, many of which are now displayed in the Museum Room. Chartwell was no longer simply the family home of a leading politician. It had become a national shrine. Admirers – from sovereigns to schoolboys – now made the pilgrimage to

Chartwell to pay their respects to the greatest living Englishman. Churchill was flattered by these attentions, and happy to be at Chartwell, but he was not ready to retire from the political fray. Speaking in Fulton, Missouri, in March 1946, he crystallised the realities of the new, Cold War in a single sentence: 'From Stettin in the Baltic to Trieste in the Adriatic, an iron curtain has descended across the Continent.'[5] And he saw battles still to be won in the House of Commons, which rose restored from the ashes of wartime devastation in October 1950. A year later, with 'a willing, eager heart' he fought his sixteenth election campaign and became Prime Minister once again.[6] At Chartwell Macmillan witnessed scenes reminiscent of the old days: 'Children, friends, Ministers, private secretaries, typists, all in a great flurry but all thoroughly enjoying the return to the centre of the stage.'[7]

In wartime Churchill had steadied the nation's nerve by the sheer power of his oratory. Now he

33

In old age Churchill was fond of sitting by the fish pond feeding his golden orfe; he painted this view in the 1930s (private collection)

was determined to bring back a mood of optimism after the grey years of austerity. Symbolic of the new era was the Coronation in 1953. Clementine described her husband, only half in jest, as the last believer in the divine right of kings. He had an almost mystic conception of British history, and of the place of the monarchy at the heart of it. Nothing made him prouder than to stand in Westminster Abbey, wearing the Garter insignia of the 1st Duke, as first minister to a new, young queen.

Even Churchill's boundless energy and strong constitution could not hold back the years for ever. Three weeks after the Coronation he suffered a massive stroke and was taken down to Chartwell to recover; despite his serious condition he was defiant. The Cabinet Secretary, Lord Normanbrook, recalled an evening at Chartwell shortly afterwards:

Colville [Churchill's Principal Private Secretary] and I dined with him alone. He was in a wheelchair. After dinner, in the drawing-room, he said that he was going to stand on his feet. Colville and I urged him not to attempt this, and, when he insisted, we came up on either side of him so that we could catch him if he fell. But he waved us away with his stick and told us to stand back. He then lowered his feet to the ground, gripped the arms of his chair, and by a tremendous effort – with sweat pouring down his face – levered himself to his feet and stood upright. Having demonstrated that he could do this, he sat down again and took up his cigar.[8]

Having conquered this affliction and lost none of his appetite for 'a square meal and a pint of champagne', Churchill finally and reluctantly retired in April 1955, at the age of 80. The burdens and exhilaration of power were gone, but he was by now a public institution and there was much still to be done, with the help of his devoted private secretary, Anthony Montague Browne: letters to be answered, speeches to be given; and not the least the foundation of a science-based college in Cambridge that was to bear his name and preserve his huge personal archive. The Churchills could spend more time relaxing in the Chartwell garden or in the sunshine of the south of France. Their golden wedding anniversary in 1958 was celebrated at Lord Beaverbrook's villa at Cap d'Ail, La Capponcina. To mark the occasion, their children gave them golden-flowering roses, which filled the borders of a new walk in the garden, and were painted by some of the leading artists of the day. The handsome folio containing these illustrations now sits in the Dining Room.

Churchill's last years were spent painting by the lake or in a game of bezique over whisky and soda with Clementine or close friends. Only the growing brood of grandchildren disturbed the general quiet. Gradually the torrent of words, written and spoken, slowed. He would sit in silence for hours by the fishpond, feeding his golden orfe and meditating. 40 years before, he had written to Clementine after the death of her mother: 'An old & failing life going out on the tide, after the allotted span has been spent & after most joys have faded is not a case for human pity.'[9]

When Churchill died in 1965, schools and factories closed, and the nation came to a halt. On a bitterly cold January day his body was carried slowly through the streets of London to the state funeral at St Paul's, then up the Thames and through the Oxfordshire countryside to Bladon. In an empty field a farmhand stood alone, head bowed, cap in hand, as the funeral train passed by. From the roof of Chartwell the standard of the Lord Warden of the Cinque Ports flew at half-mast.

A plaque in Westminster Abbey bears this simple request:

REMEMBER WINSTON CHURCHILL

On 22 June 1966 Chartwell was opened to the public for the first time by the National Trust. Grace Hamblin agreed to become the first administrator. With the generous help of Lady Churchill and Mary Soames, furniture was reorganised, faded curtains renewed, and the walls hung with many of Churchill's paintings. In the garden Lanning Roper supervised the restoration of the old planting and created new borders in the same spirit. Chartwell was gradually returned to its pre-war appearance – to the years when a family home in Kent was a symbol of opposition to tyranny and the most important country house in Europe.

NOTES

1 Quoted Brendon, 1984, p.199.

2 CC/Captain George Spencer-Churchill, 30 October 1945. Quoted Gilbert, *VIII. Never Despair, 1945–1965*, 1988, p.164.

3 WSC/Camrose, 29 December 1945. Camrose papers. Quoted Gilbert, *VIII. Never Despair, 1945–1965*, 1988, p.176.

4 Quoted Gilbert *VIII. Never Despair, 1945–1965*, 1988, p.488, n.2.

5 Ibid., p.200.

6 Ibid., p.650.

7 Macmillan, 1969, pp.364–5.

8 Wheeler-Bennett, 1968, pp.43–4.

9 WSC/CC, 22 March 1925. Spencer-Churchill papers. Quoted Gilbert, *Companion*, V, i, 1979, p.445.

CHAPTER SIX

CHURCHILL THE WRITER

In 1897, at the age of 23, Churchill wrote his one and only novel, *Savrola*, a Ruritanian tale of politics and romance in the style of *The Prisoner of Zenda*. The hero, Savrola, is both an idealised portrait of Churchill's father and a projection of all that the ambitious young army officer wished to become. Savrola's book-lined study is filled with the works of Churchill's favourite authors, including Gibbon, Macaulay and Dr Johnson:

A broad writing-table occupied the place of honour. It was arranged so that the light fell conveniently to hand and head. A large bronze ink-stand formed the centre-piece, with a voluminous blotting-pad of simple manufacture spread open before it. The rest of the table was occupied by papers or files. The floor, in spite of the ample waste-paper basket, was littered with scraps. It was the writing-table of a public man.[1]

When Churchill came to rebuild Chartwell, he made sure that just such a writing-table – inherited from his father – stood in the Study, from which poured a constant stream of books, speeches, news-paper articles, letters and memos.

Writing was always central to Churchill's life. He claimed, somewhat misleadingly, to have learnt little at school, but there he did at least begin to absorb the great histories of Gibbon, Macaulay and Lecky, which became his passion as a young subaltern in India. And more importantly, at Harrow 'I got into my bones the essential structure of the ordinary British sentence – which is a noble thing.'[2] In his youth Churchill somehow managed to combine an army career with journalism, to the irritation of the military authorities. He pulled strings to get a ringside seat wherever the action was hottest and likely to yield the most exciting copy. Churchill never lost the journalist's desire to be on the spot when history was being made. It took the intervention of the King to dissuade him from joining the invasion fleet during the Normandy

landings in June 1944. Churchill also had a journal-ist's respect for deadlines, although he often cut it very fine. While negotiating the contract for *The Story of the Malakand Field Force*, which described his adventures on the North-West Frontier in 1897, he made the agreeable discovery that writing could pay: in two months he earned as much as he had done in two years as a subaltern. At that date anyone with Churchill's political ambitions needed outside means, and from then on he depended very heavily on his literary earnings to support a lavish lifestyle.

Although Churchill was Chancellor of the Ex-chequer during his first five years at Chartwell, he still found time to write the final two volumes of his history of the First World War, *The World Crisis*, and its sequel covering the following four years, *The Aftermath*. When the Baldwin government fell in May 1929, Churchill needed money and had the leisure to write much more. Two weeks after the election defeat he signed the contract for *Marl-borough: His Life and Times*, which was published in four volumes between 1933 and 1938. The project had been in his mind for years, as he revered the great soldier Duke. In many ways it is his finest book: it contains much of his best writing and it embodies most clearly his conception of history.

For Churchill history was essentially the doings of great men. He believed in heroes and found them most frequently among the great military comman-ders of the past: busts of Napoleon and Nelson enjoyed honoured places on his writing-table. In *The Aftermath* he had written that 'the story of the human race is War'.[3] Warfare is the central theme of *Marlborough* and it was the great issues of war and peace that most concerned him as a politician.

History was also very much a family affair, and according to Churchill's research assistant, Maurice Ashley, 'to him the writing of history was to be first and foremost an act of piety towards his ancestors,

Churchill's desk in the Study

towards his parents, even towards himself.'[4] In 1906 he had published *Lord Randolph Churchill* to resurrect his father's shattered political reputation. Thereafter most of his books had Churchill or the Churchill family at their heart. In these circumstances it was hardly surprising that he made no pretence of being objective. In *Marlborough* he analyses the political machinations of life at the English court with a politician's insight, but the case he presents for the 1st Duke is that of the defence counsel, in rebuttal of Macaulay's hostile account. He glosses over John Churchill's betrayal of James II in 1688 and attempts to explain away his rampant greed. As Churchill blithely told Ashley, 'Give me the facts, and I will twist them the way I want to suit my argument.'[5]

Churchill always looked back at the past from the perspective of the present. The past also cast a long shadow: history might not repeat itself, but it still contained warnings to be heeded. Writing in the preface to the third volume of *Marlborough* in 1936, he pointed up the parallels he saw between Louis XIV and Hitler: 'We see a world war of a league of Nations against a mighty, central military monarchy, hungering for domination not only over the lands but over the politics and religion of its neighbours. We see in their extremes the feebleness and selfish shortcomings of a numerous coalition.'[6] In 1939 Churchill sent a copy of the book to the American President, Franklin Roosevelt, who much enjoyed reading it. Central to Churchill's story is the partnership of Marlborough and his great wartime ally, Prince Eugene of Savoy, the 'Twin Captains' of the Grand Alliance. The historical echoes must have rung loud in Churchill's ears and encouraged him to foster his special relationship with Roosevelt, which did so much to ensure allied victory over Hitler.

Churchill managed to write so much because of his unusual methods of working.[7] For major projects like *Marlborough* he employed a bright young history graduate as a research assistant. Maurice Ashley and later William Deakin both worked for Churchill in this capacity in the 1930s and became very much part of life at Chartwell. The material they ferreted out from the Blenheim archives was laid out on the lectern in the Study, so that Churchill could consult it as he stomped up and down the room, puffing on his cigar and dictating in gruff, almost inaudible tones to his secretary. When he got into the swing, the words rolled out with matchless fluency. On other occasions he would stop and start awkwardly, but he generally

managed at least 3,000 words during a midnight session. Dictation gave to all his work the immediacy of the spoken word – sometimes rhetorical, but often rich in irony and honest passion. He tried using a dictaphone when they were first introduced. However, the cumbersome earlier models prevented him from walking up and down, which he found essential, and he soon reverted to using a secretary with rapid shorthand or later a noiseless typewriter. Almost before the sheets had been typed, Churchill grabbed them from the machine and began the long process of revision. When he had the text ready to his own satisfaction, it would be set in type and circulated to numerous friends and specialist advisers, who would check it for accuracy, elegance of expression and grammar. In those more generous days his publisher often allowed him to revise the proofs as many as six times.

Churchill's speeches were prepared in the Study with the same care. After an embarrassing early experience when he dried up in public, he always dictated full notes of what he wanted to say beforehand, using phrases and ideas he had tried out first on guests around the Dining Room table at Chartwell. His words were typed up on octavo sheets held together with green treasury tags (he abominated paper clips), and were laid out in a

Churchill consulting reference books at the lectern in the Study. He much preferred to work standing up

Churchill's war memoirs were translated into every major language

peculiar kind of blank verse, with phrases, even individual words, on separate lines, and the pauses and breath marks all carefully indicated. A sense of history, a love of words and meticulous preparation all went into the famous speeches which gave voice to the national mood of defiance in 1940:

This wicked man, the repository and embodiment of many forms of soul-destroying hatreds, this monstrous product of former wrongs and shame, has now resolved to try to break our famous Island race by a process of indiscriminate slaughter and destruction. What he has done is to kindle a fire in British hearts, here and all over the world, which will glow long after all traces of the conflagration he has caused in London have been removed. He has lighted a fire which will burn with a steady and consuming flame until the last vestiges of Nazi tyranny have been burnt out of Europe, and until the Old World – and the New – can join hands to rebuild the temples of man's freedom and man's honour, upon foundations which will not soon or easily be overthrown.[8]

NOTES

1 *Savrola*, Longman, 1900, p.40.

2 *My Early Life*, 1930, p.31.

3 *The Aftermath*, 1929, p.451.

4 Ashley, 1968, p.13.

5 Ibid., p.18.

6 *Marlborough: His Life and Times*, III, 1936, p.19.

7 See Mary Thompson, 'Secretary to Churchill', in Eade, 1953.

8 Broadcast of 11 September 1940. Quoted Gilbert, 1991, pp.675–6.

CHAPTER SEVEN

CHURCHILL THE PAINTER

by Mary Soames

Painting and Winston Churchill discovered each other by accident when he was 41. This new ploy, which was to become an engrossing occupation for the rest of his active life, took the role of a therapy, distracting his mind from the traumatic debacle of the 1915 Dardanelles campaign, in the planning of which he was deeply involved. During the summer months of that fateful year, Winston and Clementine rented a house, Hoe Farm, near Godalming in Surrey; and to this haven with its charming garden and peaceful surroundings they retreated at weekends with their family. Wandering in the garden

Detail of self-portrait, 1919–20 (C31; Studio)

one day, sunk in gloomy broodings, Winston came upon his sister-in-law, Goonie, painting. She encouraged him to try for himself, and, as he seemed intrigued, she commandeered her young son's box of watercolours. After brief experimentation with these, Winston soon embarked on a canvas with oil paints, the medium in which he worked hereafter. This was the beginning of his long love affair with the Muse of Painting.

By providential coincidence expert teachers were at hand to aid Winston's early efforts: the Irish portrait painter Sir John Lavery and his wife Hazel, herself a gifted artist, happened to be London neighbours of the Churchills, and, urgently summoned by their friends, they motored to Hoe Farm where Lady Lavery took the budding artist in hand. Churchill has described what followed:

'Painting! But what are you hesitating about? Let me have a brush – the big one.' Splash into the turpentine, wallop into the blue and the white, frantic flourish on the palette – clean no longer – and then several large, fierce strokes and slashes of blue on the absolutely cowering canvas. Anyone could see that it could not hit back. No evil fate avenged the jaunty violence. The canvas grinned in helplessness before me. The spell was broken. The sickly inhibitions rolled away. I seized the largest brush and fell upon my victim with Berserk fury. I have never felt any awe of a canvas since.[1]

One of the pictures Churchill painted at this date now hangs in the Studio.

From this time on, painting was to form an essential part of Winston's life. He rarely now left home on visits (whether for duty or pleasure) without his artist's impedimenta. He even took his paints to Flanders in November 1915, when serving in the trenches where he painted the stricken surroundings of his Battalion's headquarters. One of these scenes, of the village of Ploegsteert, painted under shell-fire, hangs on the first-floor landing.

Two glasses on a verandah (after Sargent), 1926 (C179; Lady Churchill's Sitting Room)

Having discovered this fascinating new occupation in middle age, Winston felt he had no time to lose, and consequently he never submitted himself to the academic apprenticeship of learning to draw. He was largely self-taught, but profited from the valuable advice of several notable artists. After Lavery, the next major (although indirect) influence on Winston's painting was the American painter John Singer Sargent, whose work he studied and admired in the collection of his friend Sir Philip Sassoon (a great art connoisseur, who was a patron of Sargent). Sir Philip would allow Winston to borrow pictures so he might copy them as learning practice. *Two glasses on a verandah* (C179; Lady Churchill's Sitting Room) and *The Ruins of Arras Cathedral* are particularly fine examples of Churchill's paintings after Sargent.

For about two years from 1927 Winston saw a good deal of W. R. Sickert. He had been a friend of Clementine's mother, and knew Clementine herself as a schoolgirl. He came back into her life again quite by chance at this time, and he and Winston took instantly to each other. During long sessions, either at Chartwell or No. 11 Downing Street, Sickert conveyed much of his knowledge and technique to his eager pupil. Winston absorbed a great deal from his enjoyable association with Sickert, particularly with regard to the preparation of canvases, and the handling and laying on of paint. He taught Winston among other things the use of the 'magic lantern' to throw magnified photographs on to the canvas, and how photographs could help in composing and recalling painting subjects – methods which Churchill was still using into the forties and fifties. *Tea at Chartwell* (C36; Dining Room Passage) is one of several pictures at Chartwell painted in this way. Sickert himself appears seated at the extreme right.

After the defeat of Baldwin's Conservative government in 1929, Churchill was to be out of office for ten years – a memorable decade, called in the terms of his career and life the Wilderness Years, but in many ways a flowering wilderness. Apart from politics which then – as always – dominated

Tea at Chartwell, c.1928 (C36; Dining Room Passage)

Marrakesh,
1935–6 (C81;
Inner Hall)

his time and energy, those ten years saw his literary and artistic output at floodtide.

During the thirties two very different artists (both in terms of their art and personalities) were frequent visitors to Chartwell: Paul Maze,[2] a well-known French painter, who lived for the most part in England, and William Nicholson. Both Maze and Nicholson were marvellous companions of the brush for Winston, and had their influence on his painting. While staying at Chartwell around 1933 Nicholson painted the view of the front door which now hangs in the Hall. About the same time he also painted the Churchills at breakfast (Dining Room).

Although Winston was always eager to be taught by what he called 'real artists', he developed his own manner of painting quite early on in his painting career. Outside influences, to a greater or lesser extent, joined the mainstream of his own natural style. Professor Thomas Bodkin wrote that Churchill was an 'instinctive painter, though one who is always searching for fresh ways and means to produce the desired results.'[3] Churchill always found much pleasure in painting in the south of France, loving the brilliant light and glorious colours (C131; Inner Hall). He also discovered

Marrakesh in Morocco (C81; Inner Hall), and stayed there in the Mamounia Hotel on many occasions both before and after the Second World War. And Chartwell of course, supplied many 'paintatious' (his adjective) scenes, like his famous swimming pool. Forced indoors by wintry weather, he would paint the snowy garden and Weald from the Drawing Room windows.

With the outbreak of the Second World War in 1939, brushes, paints and easel were laid aside, and Chartwell and the Studio shut up. But one picture came from Churchill's brush in the war years – a view of the city of Marrakesh painted after the Casablanca Conference in January 1943 and presented to President Roosevelt. Immediately after the war and in the wake of his humiliating and crushing defeat in the 1945 General Election, Winston took up his brushes again. At a dark moment in his fortunes 30 years before, painting had consoled and distracted him; now once more he found solace painting at Field-Marshal Alexander's villa on Lake Como (C383; Drawing Room).

In 1925 Churchill had entered one of his pictures in an amateur art competition of some standing in London. The conditions of entry ensured the entries

Winter sunshine, Chartwell, 1924–5 (C142; private collection)

were unsigned, and no clue given as to their provenance. The three artistically distinguished judges awarded the first prize to Churchill, who was naturally greatly gratified and encouraged by this unexpected success and nod of approval for his ability as a painter. Twenty-three years later he would be awarded a greater and more gleaming accolade: in 1947, at the suggestion of Sir Alfred Munnings, the President of the Royal Academy, Winston submitted three of his paintings, under the pseudonym of David Winter, to the Selection Committee for the Summer Exhibition. Only after they had been accepted was David Winter's true identity revealed. Much encouraged, Winston entered three more paintings the following year, which were again accepted: this time he used his own name. A little later the Royal Academy elected

him an Honorary Academician Extraordinary: needless to say Winston was intensely gratified. Thereafter he regularly sent paintings to the Summer Exhibitions, as all Academicians are entitled to do. And in 1959 he received the distinction of having a one-man show in the Diploma Gallery of the Royal Academy.

All these marks of praise and approval of course gave Winston enormous pleasure, but he remained (as he always had been) genuinely modest about his achievements as a painter. He painted for pure enjoyment, although he was immensely pleased if people admired 'my little daubs' – as he called them. For him painting was a fascinating adventure of endless challenges; an engrossing occupation which concentrated his mind on quite other problems: proportion, gradations of colours, light and shade, the limpidity of water.

Of some 500 Churchill paintings extant today, around 125 can be seen at Chartwell, forming a colourful setting to the events and circumstances of his long life. He was principally a landscape painter, but there are also many interior scenes, still lifes and flower studies (C382, *Buddha and scarlet hippeastrum*, Hall; C154, *Magnolia*, First Floor Landing). He even made brave ventures into portrait painting (*Sir Archibald Sinclair*; *Lady Castlerosse*, both Inner Studio). In 1954 he produced his first and only sculpture – a head of Oscar Nemon, the sculptor for whom he sat in latter years. The original plaster cast stands in the Studio beside his easel.

In 1921 Churchill had written two articles for the *Strand Magazine* entitled 'Painting as a Pastime'. Later, in 1948, they were published as a small book of the same title. It is pure enchantment to read, throbbing as it does with enthusiasm, and giving encouragement to others to seize brush and canvas and 'have a go', as Churchill himself had done:

We must not be too ambitious. We cannot aspire to masterpieces. We may content ourselves with a joy ride in a paint-box. And for this Audacity is the only ticket.

And again:

Just to paint is great fun. The colours are lovely to look at and delicious to squeeze out. Matching them,

however crudely, with what you see is fascinating and absolutely absorbing. Try it if you have not done so – before you die.[5]

Churchill unashamedly declared his allegiance to bright colours:

I rejoice with the brilliant ones, and am genuinely sorry for the poor browns. When I get to heaven I mean to spend a considerable portion of my first million years in painting, and so get to the bottom of the subject. But then I shall require a still gayer palette than I get here below. I expect orange and vermilion will be the darkest, dullest colours upon it, and beyond them there will be a whole range of wonderful new colours which will delight the celestial eye.[6]

And looking at a collection of his paintings one receives such a strong impression of his zest for life, and the happiness and satisfaction he 'received during more than forty years by applying paint to canvas with a bold and joyous brush'.[7]

In 'Painting as a Pastime', Churchill wrote what might be regarded as an epitaph for all painters, and which happily was to prove prophetic for him:

Happy are the painters, for they shall not be lonely. Light and colour, peace and hope, will keep them company to the end, or almost to the end, of the day.[8]

NOTES

1 *Painting as a Pastime*, 1948, p.17.

2 Born in Le Havre, 1887; died in England, 1979. Educated both in France and England. Served in the First World War as unofficial liaison officer with Royal Scots Greys. Decorated DCM and MM, also Legion d'Honneur and Croix de Guerre. Wrote *A Frenchman in Khaki*, 1934.

3 'Churchill the artist' in Eade, 1953, p.424.

4 Op. cit., p.16.

5 Ibid., p.19.

6 Ibid., pp.24–5.

7 From the foreword to the catalogue of the 1959 Royal Academy exhibition by Sir Charles Wheeler, PRA.

8 Op. cit., p.13.

Churchill's brushes

PLANS OF THE HOUSE

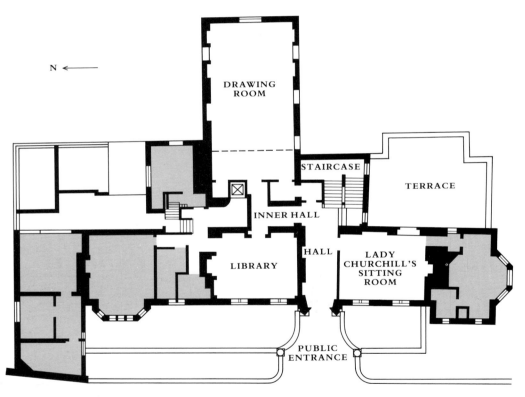

N ←

DRAWING ROOM

STAIRCASE

TERRACE

INNER HALL

HALL

LIBRARY

LADY CHURCHILL'S SITTING ROOM

PUBLIC ENTRANCE

GROUND FLOOR

Shaded areas not open to the public

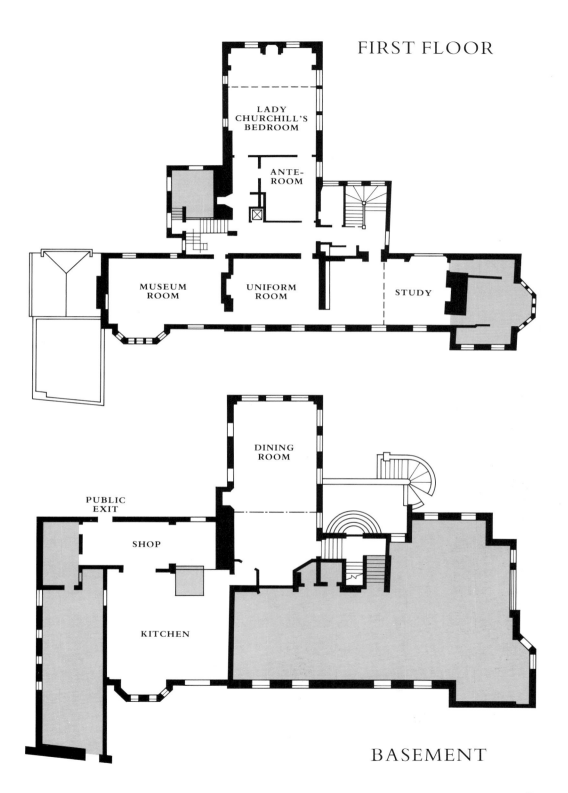

FIRST FLOOR

LADY CHURCHILL'S BEDROOM

ANTE-ROOM

MUSEUM ROOM

UNIFORM ROOM

STUDY

DINING ROOM

PUBLIC EXIT

SHOP

KITCHEN

BASEMENT

CHAPTER EIGHT
TOUR OF THE HOUSE

THE HALL

The 'panelled lounge hall' described in the 1921 sale details was swept away during Tilden's remodelling of the house. The entrance hall that he created is surprisingly narrow and modest for such a substantial house, but immediately strikes the note of domestic intimacy that characterises Chartwell. This mood is greatly enhanced by the glazed double doors, which were installed by Lady Churchill after the war to keep out the draughts.

PICTURES

(Pictures are by Churchill and in oil on canvas unless otherwise indicated. Numbers with the C prefix

Buddha and scarlet hippeastrum, 1948 (C382; Hall)

refer to David Coombs, *Churchill: His Paintings*, Hamish Hamilton, 1967.)

LEFT OF DOOR:

C382 *Buddha and scarlet hippeastrum*, 1948
The Burmese statue was bequeathed in 1947 by General Sir Ian Hamilton, British commander during the ill-fated Gallipoli campaign (1915–16), which Churchill conceived. The hippeastrum was a get-well present to Churchill from Princess Marina, Duchess of Kent, after he had caught bronchitis while staying out late, painting in the cold winter evenings of Marrakesh.

RIGHT-HAND WALL:

WILLIAM NICHOLSON, 1872–1949
The front door of Chartwell
A monochrome preparation for a painting probably done while Nicholson was staying at Chartwell in the 1930s. Nicholson gave Churchill advice with his painting, admiring the 'bold and buccaneering way' he attacked the canvas.

LEFT-HAND WALL:

BARON ISIDORE OPSOMER, 1878–1967
The port of Antwerp
Signed and dated 1945
Given by 'the grateful citizens of Antwerp', which was liberated by British troops on 4 September 1944.

SCULPTURE

HERBERT HASELTINE, 1877–1962
The Thoroughbred Horse
Signed, dated 1949, and inscribed 'To Winston Churchill'.

VISITORS' BOOK

The book records the constant stream of visitors to Chartwell, from the moment the Churchills arrived in April 1924, until the eve of the Second World War, when they moved back to London and government: a mixture of family, friends and the political allies and advisers who supported Churchill during the 'Wilderness Years'. The record resumes in January 1946, after Churchill's fall from power, and continues until October 1964, when he went up to London for his 90th birthday, never to return. The signature of 'Montgomery of Alamein', the mastermind of Churchill's greatest victories, recurs frequently in the later pages.

FURNITURE

Panelled oak chest.

English wall-mirror in walnut frame, early eighteenth-century style.

Mahogany umbrella stand, containing a number of Churchill's walking sticks, including an aluminium shooting-stick, which Churchill used in old age when walking around the garden.

THE LOBBY

PICTURES

NEVILLE LYTTON, 1879–1951
*Mrs Bertram Romilly in fancy dress, c.*1910
Lady Churchill's sister and a frequent visitor to Chartwell.

JOHN SINGER SARGENT, RA, 1856–1925
Winston Churchill
Charcoal
Dated 1925
Churchill is shown wearing the Chancellor of the Exchequer's robes that had belonged to his father, who had briefly held the post in 1886. Churchill was appointed Chancellor in October 1924, shortly after the family moved to Chartwell.

THE DRAWING ROOM

This is one of the three principal rooms in the projecting east wing that Churchill had Tilden add to the house and which he christened 'my promontory'. Windows on three sides give the room a light and airy feel, and provide views south over the garden and the Weald of Kent. The decoration, particularly the flower-patterned glazed chintz curtains, reflects Lady Churchill's taste, and dates from the 1950s.

The Drawing Room was the main meeting place

Some of Churchill's large collection of walking sticks

for the family and their guests. It was originally rather longer, but was shortened when the lift was installed. The room was briefly used as a studio after the Second World War, but soon reverted to its present appearance.

PICTURES

C383 *Lakeside Scene, Lake Como,* 1945
After his defeat at the general election in the summer of 1945, Churchill went to stay and paint at Field-Marshal Alexander's villa on Lake Como.

C259 *The Italian garden, Hever, c.*1930
Churchill painted several pictures at Hever Castle, J.J. (later Lord) Astor's ancient house near Chartwell.

C317 *The Surf Club at Miami, c.*1946

DOUGLAS CHANDOR, 1874–1965
Lady Churchill, 1946
This American artist also painted Churchill, in RAF uniform, in 1946 (now National Portrait Gallery, Washington).

C319 *Coastal scene*

OVER CHIMNEY-PIECE:

RAOUL MILLAIS, b.1901
Colonist II, 1951
Churchill loved horses. In his youth he was a cavalry officer and keen polo player; he also much enjoyed

riding to hounds. After the Second World War he became a racehorse owner and from 1949 his horses were trained by Walter Nightingall with considerable success. Colonist II, a French-bred colt, was bought as a maiden three-year-old and won many valuable races.

C298 *A Study of Boats*
Painted on the French Riviera, around 1933.

C6 *Roses, c.*1928

CLAUDE MONET, 1840–1926
Charing Cross Bridge
Signed and dated 1902
Monet began his series of Thames views while staying at the Savoy in autumn 1899; many were painted from the hotel balcony. The challenge of capturing the foggy London atmosphere of the period clearly fascinated him, as he returned in early 1900 and 1901. However, this picture, which is unfinished, was probably painted from memory in his studio at Giverny. It was given to Churchill by Emery Reves, who bought the lucrative foreign rights to his books after the Second World War, and with whom he often stayed in later years in the south of France.

C361 *River Scene on the Loup, c.*1930

SCULPTURE

RIGHT OF ENTRANCE DOOR:
Small marble bust of Napoleon.

FURNITURE AND CERAMICS

IN LEFT-HAND BOOKCASE:
One piece from the set of nineteenth-century Dresden figures shown in Lady Churchill's Bedroom.

ON CHIMNEY-PIECE:
A pair of Paris wine coolers, late eighteenth-century.

A Russian enamelled silver box, in the form of a coffer.

BESIDE FAR SOFA:
Mahogany tripod table with 'pie-crust' border. On it is a silver match-holder inscribed with Churchill's initials and given by his daughter Sarah at Christmas 1953.

The armchair nearby was Churchill's favourite.

Mahogany fold-over card table, on which stands a crystal glass cockerel, by Lalique. This symbol of France was given to Lady Churchill by General Charles de Gaulle.

BEYOND SOFA:

Georgian mahogany card table, set for bezique with a deck of cards bearing Churchill's signature. He was an avid player of the game in his later years. Bezique and backgammon took over from mah jong, which was the fashionable game in the 1920s.

EITHER SIDE OF FAR (EAST) WINDOW:

Two mirrors of George II design. Below them is a pair of mid-eighteenth-century walnut side-tables, whose tops are inlaid with medallions in satinwood. The blue vases mounted as lamps are Chinese, K'ang Hsi period (1662–1722).

Pair of Louis XV embroidered armchairs. One was presented to Churchill with the Freedom of Brighton, the other bought later by Lady Churchill to match.

Regency black lacquer table with Chinoiserie decoration, which may have come from the Brighton Pavilion.

UNDER MONET:

Mahogany *bureau à cylindre* in Louis XVI style. Upon it stands a mid-nineteenth-century Staffordshire group of St George and the Dragon.

Mahogany Pembroke table banded in satinwood, the top inlaid with the arms of the City of Worcester, which gave the table to Churchill, when he received the Freedom of that city.

CARPET

The large boldly patterned Persian carpet is a nineteenth-century Mahal, bought by the Churchills in the 1950s.

THE INNER HALL

PICTURES

JOHN PINE, 1690–1756
The Chamber of the House of Commons, 1741/2
Hand-coloured engraving, dedicated to Speaker Onslow, 1747
'The House of Commons has ever been the controller and, if need be, the changer of the rulers of the day and of the Ministers appointed by the Crown. It stands for ever against oligarchy and one-man power.' (Churchill, October 1950.)

Painted shield
The interior of the House of Commons was destroyed by enemy bombs in May 1941. This shield is thought to be the sole surviving relic.

The Drawing Room

SAMUEL COUSINS, 1801–87, after H. W. BURGESS, fl.1809–44
The Chamber of the House of Commons
Aquatint, 1835

CHARLES SIMS, RA, 1873–1928
Diana and Sarah Churchill as girls
Painted in 1922. Churchill had reservations about the picture, thinking it made Diana look 'priggish' and Sarah 'rather impudent'.

C81 *Marrakesh, c.*1935

C113 *Remains of a Greek Temple, doorway and pillars, c.*1926

C131 *Harbour in the South of France, c.*1925

THE LIBRARY

One might expect such a master of the written and spoken word to have built himself a more imposing library. Churchill revered books as material objects and as the distillation of a nation's history. He loved to be surrounded by books, and received many as

The Library

presents, but he bought them chiefly as practical tools for a working historian and journalist. An exception was his fine collection of books on Napoleon, which was given after his death by Lady Churchill to Churchill College, Cambridge. Churchill always worked and wrote in his first-floor Study, where he kept the books he referred to most frequently.

RELIEF MODEL

The model inset into the bookshelves on the left shows the artificial harbour of Port Arromanches in Normandy, as it appeared on D-Day plus 109 days (23 September 1944). In the months leading up to D-Day (6 June) Churchill was much involved in the design of the artificial 'Mulberry harbours', which played a vital part in supplying the allied landing forces during the critical early days of the invasion of Europe.

PICTURES

BYZANTINE, nineteenth-century
St John the Baptist
An icon given to Churchill by Archbishop Damaskinos, head of the Greek Orthodox Church, when he visited Athens in the winter of 1944, shortly after the withdrawal of the German forces.

FRANK O. SALISBURY, 1874–1962
Winston Churchill, 1942
Churchill is shown seated at his desk in one of the blue 'Siren Suits' that he favoured during the war. A later example is shown in the Uniform Room.

SCULPTURE

JO DAVIDSON, 1883–1952
Franklin Delano Roosevelt (1882–1945)
This bust of Churchill's great wartime ally was given by Averell Harriman, who came to Britain in 1941 as Roosevelt's special envoy and became a friend of the Churchills.

'Roaring Meg'
Scale model of the cannon which played an important part in the siege of Londonderry in 1688–9. It was presented to Churchill when he was given the Freedom of the city in 1955.

FURNITURE

Mirror in an elaborate Italian seventeenth-century giltwood frame.

On the writing desk below are signed photographs

Seascape at Sunset, 1920s (C103; Staircase)

of King George VI and Queen Elizabeth. The official Coronation photograph of Queen Elizabeth II is by Cecil Beaton, and is signed by her.

BEHIND DOOR:

An elephant-size dispatch box. It stood on the table of the House of Lords (to which the Commons transferred after it was bombed out of its own chamber) from June 1941 until October 1950, when it was presented to Churchill.

CARPET

Persian carpet, woven in Tabriz.

THE STAIRCASE

The stairs were installed in 1966 to replace the original stairs, which were judged too cramped to take the number of visitors anticipated when the house was opened to the public.

CARTOONS

The walls are decorated with cartoons by David Low and E. H. Shepherd. The climax of Churchill's career coincided with one of the great ages of the political cartoon, and his achievements provided a fertile source of inspiration for Low and his con-

temporaries. Edward Ardizzone's drawing shows Churchill at the dispatch box of the House of Commons, and was presented by the Parliamentary Press Club on his eightieth birthday in 1954.

PHOTOGRAPHS

The photographs feature some of Churchill's closest political colleagues and friends, including Lady Violet Bonham-Carter, the Earl of Birkenhead, Lord Kitchener, Admiral of the Fleet Lord Fisher and H. H. Asquith.

PICTURES

C377 *Buddha and Lily*, 1948
Painted at the same time as the version of the same subject in the Hall (C382).

C103 *Seascape at Sunset*, 1920s

THE FIRST FLOOR CORRIDOR

PICTURE

C386 *Fontaine de Vaucluse*, 1948

SCULPTURE

OSCAR NEMON, 1906–85
Winston Churchill
Plaster maquette for the life-size statue of Churchill in the Members' Lobby of the House of Commons.

Lady Churchill's Bedroom

LADY CHURCHILL'S BEDROOM

This room was added to the house when Tilden built his new garden wing. The high barrel-vaulted ceiling, duck egg blue colour scheme and the usually white flowers which Lady Churchill preferred, all add to the sense of space and calm. Churchill called it 'a magnificent aerial bower.' Lady Churchill spent many hours here, dealing with her correspondence and the household accounts at the writing desk, and interviewing her staff. When the house was reorganised following the Churchills' return after the war, it became a dining-room for a brief period.

The eighteenth-century stone fireplace was introduced by Tilden when the room was built.

LEFT-HAND (NORTH) WALL:
ENGLISH SCHOOL?, mid-nineteenth-century
Two unknown women looking at a letter
Chalk drawing

After EDWARD CLIFFORD, 1844–1907
Henrietta Blanche Stanley, Countess of Airlie
(1830–1921)
Reproduction of a drawing of Lady Churchill's grandmother, signed and dated May 1891.

SARAH CHURCHILL, 1914–82
The artist's Malibu beach chalet by day and
by moonlight, 1957
Two watercolours (heightened with bodycolour and pastel).

After JOHN MERTON, b.1913
Sarah Churchill (1914–82), c.1933

Sir JOHN TENNIEL, 1820–1914
Churchill as a boy, 1890
Pencil drawing

LEFT OF FIREPLACE, ABOVE:

After G. F. WATTS, RA, 1817–1904
*Henrietta Blanche Stanley, Countess of Airlie
(1830–1921),* 1866
A reproduction of Watt's painting of Lady Churchill's grandmother in Renaissance dress.

BELOW:

Photographs of Churchill; his daughter Mary
Soames, with her two eldest children, Nicholas and
Emma; and his granddaughter Celia Sandys.

ON CIRCULAR TABLE:

Photograph of Randolph Churchill with his second
wife, June Osborne, and their daughter Arabella.

RIGHT OF FIREPLACE, ABOVE:

CHARLES-LOUIS GEOFFROY-DECHAUME, 1877–
after 1961
Diana Churchill, Mrs Duncan Sandys (1909–63)
Chalk drawing

BELOW:

Photographs of Sarah, later Lady Audley; and of
Oswald Birley's painting of Sarah, later Lady
Soames, as a girl.

Pencil drawing of Blanche Hosier, Lady Churchill's
mother.

FURNITURE AND FURNISHINGS

A late seventeenth-century walnut *armoire*, probably Italian, its front treated classically with cornice, fluted pilasters and Ionic capitals.

ABOVE CHIMNEY-PIECE:

A mid-eighteenth-century gilt gesso mirror.

ON CHIMNEY-PIECE:

A cylindrical Louis XVI clock surmounted by an
eagle, made by Gavelle the elder, *c.*1780. It belonged
to Churchill's mother.

CENTRE OF ROOM:

A mahogany knee-hole writing desk, at which
stands a Regency chair with 'sabre' legs of about
1820. On the desk is one of the last photographs
of Churchill, together with a photograph of the
Churchills' daughter, Marigold, the much-loved
'duckadilly', who died in 1921 before her third

*Porcelain figures of
Napoleon and one of
his officers, made at
the Potschappel
factory near Dresden
in 1875 (Lady
Churchill's
Bedroom)*

birthday. Lady Churchill was fond of pencils, and a box of an Italian variety sits by the blotter.

A 1920s dressing-table, covered in pleated silk to match the colour of the walls, with a six-legged painted stool. The Victorian silver-mounted crystal dressing set, engraved with cipher and coronet, belonged to the Countess of Airlie. The two cut-glass decanters with silver stoppers, engraved with a ducal coronet and the letter 'M' for Marlborough, were a post-war gift to Churchill.

BESIDE DRESSING-TABLE:

Lady Churchill's jewel case, which had belonged to the Countess of Airlie.

The four-poster bed, hung with moiré silk, is flanked by two urn-shaped French Empire bed tables made of walnut.

CERAMICS

LEFT-HAND WALL:

Blanc-de-Chine figures of the maternal goddess Kwan Yin.

IN WALL ALCOVES:

A collection of porcelain equestrian figures made at the Potschappel factory near Dresden in 1875. One represents Napoleon, and others members of the French Imperial Army. They were given to Lady Churchill by Brendan Bracken.

THE ANTE-ROOM

This small room was originally Lady Churchill's bathroom. It is now used to display china, medals and other memorabilia associated with the Churchills.

PHOTOGRAPHS AND DOCUMENTS

On the left-hand wall are signed photographs of many of the allied commanders who worked with Churchill in the Second World War.

Right of the china cabinet hangs a facsimile of Roosevelt's letter of January 1941 to 'A Certain Naval Person' (the codename Churchill, a former First Lord of the Admiralty, preferred). At this critical point in the conflict Roosevelt offered Britain a vital pledge of support; ten months later he brought the United States into the war.

On the right-hand wall is a copy of Churchill's terse directive to the British commander in the Middle East, Field-Marshall Alexander, drafted in Cairo in August 1942 and also initialled by the Chief of the Imperial General Staff, Alan Brooke, instructing him to expel the German and Italian forces from North Africa. Below it is Alexander's no less terse response, informing the Prime Minster in 1943 that the order had been successfully carried out. There are also photographs of the American financier Bernard Baruch, dated 1928, and the German Chancellor Bismarck.

CERAMICS

IN GEORGIAN MAHOGANY CABINET:

Top Shelf: A Royal Crown Derby service.

Second Shelf: A Russian tea service, dated 1945 and decorated with views of Leningrad (now St Petersburg). It was presented by the Mayor of Leningrad to Lady Churchill who visited the devastated city shortly before the end of the war on behalf of the Red Cross Aid to Russia Fund, of which she was chairman.

Third Shelf: A Dresden coffee set, richly gilded on apple-green ground, and painted with portraits of Napoleon and ladies of the French Imperial court. Many of the pieces bear the mark (the letters 'RK' with a crown) of R. Klemm, a decorator working at Dresden after 1868.

Lower shelves: Three very similar, mostly mid-nineteenth-century, Sèvres dinner services, with gilt decoration and the cipher of Napoleon III on a white ground. Many of the pieces were rescued by Churchill's maternal grandmother, Clara Jerome, from the ashes of the Tuileries palace in Paris, which was gutted by fire in May 1871 during the bitter fighting that marked the suppression of the Paris Commune. She carried them back to her apartment in the Boulevard Haussman on a hired wheelbarrow.

MEDALS

The mahogany square piano banded with satinwood, and converted into a display cabinet, houses a collection of commemorative medals, mainly associated with the Second World War.

LADY CHURCHILL'S ROBES

The glass case against the right-hand wall contains the robes of Lady Churchill, who was created Baroness Spencer-Churchill in 1965. The case also

A tea service decorated with views of Leningrad (now St Petersburg), which was presented by the mayor of the city to Lady Churchill during her visit to the Soviet Union in 1945

displays her medals, which include the Order of the Red Banner of Labour awarded to her by Stalin in recognition of her work for the Aid to Russia Fund.

THE LANDING

PICTURES

LEFT WALL:

C459 *The Todhra Gorge*
Painted in Morocco in 1951.

C154 *Magnolia*, c.1930
This is a flower from the magnificent *M. grandiflora* that grows right up to Churchill's bedroom window. He was particularly fond of the beautiful lemon-scented blooms, which he would pick and often paint.

C415 *St Jean, Cap-Ferrat*, 1946

C7 *Mallows*, c.1928

C68 *Trees by a Stream in Norfolk*, c.1923
Churchill painted many Norfolk landscapes when staying at Breccles Hall with Edwin Montagu, whose brilliant wife, Venetia Stanley, was Lady Churchill's cousin. Montagu was Secretary of State for India from 1917 to 1922.

RIGHT WALL:

C96 *Coast near Cannes*, 1925

C4 *Plug Street*, 1916
Churchill had begun to paint in the previous year.

The title is a familiar corruption of Ploegsteert near the French-Belgian border, Churchill's regimental headquarters when in command of the 6th Battalion of the Royal Scots Fusiliers in the First World War.

FURNITURE

The chairs were used by Winston and Clementine Churchill in Westminster Abbey at the coronation of King George VI in 1937.

THE MUSEUM ROOM

This room and the adjoining Uniform Room were created out of three guest bedrooms in 1966.

PHOTOGRAPHS AND DOCUMENTS

On the door is the charter proclaiming Churchill Lord Warden of the Cinque Ports.

The life-size photographs which cover two walls portray Churchill from childhood to old age. The raised photograph by the far doorway shows him from behind in dressing-gown and ten-gallon hat painting in the West Indies. (One of these distinctive hats is displayed in the next room.)

On the left of the same doorway is the notice written in Afrikaans and English offering £25 for the recapture of Churchill 'dead or alive' following his escape from a Boer prison in December 1899.

SCULPTURE

AGAINST FAR WALL:

CLARE SHERIDAN, 1885–1970
Winston Churchill, 1942
Bronze

Churchill sat for this bust by his cousin in 1942. He had been knocked over by a taxi in a New York street in 1931, and the scar he bore from the accident is still clearly visible on his forehead.

GIFTS AND AWARDS

In his later years Churchill was widely recognised as the greatest Englishman of the twentieth century, and was showered with awards and gifts by his admirers. Many of these are displayed here, most on loan from his grandson, Winston Churchill, MP. The donors range from peoples, potentates and prime ministers to corporations and societies. They include the United States of America and associations as modest as the Hastings Winkle Club, of which Churchill was a member. Among the most attractive exhibits are the two silver-gilt cups given by King George VI and Queen Elizabeth, the simple silver-gilt casket presented with the Freedom of the City of Westminster, the crystal cross of Lorraine from President de Gaulle, the green-glazed Persian pottery bowl from President Roosevelt, and the silver box designed as a shako, which Churchill received on his eightieth birthday from the officers of his old regiment, the 4th Queen's Own Hussars.

In the wall cases are his honorary American citizenship, his Nobel Prize for Literature and Oratory, awarded in 1953, and the volume which records the tribute of the House of Commons on his eightieth birthday.

THE UNIFORM ROOM

PHOTOGRAPH

On the right-hand wall between the windows a life-size photograph shows Churchill saying farewell to the Queen after she had dined with him at Downing Street on 4 April 1955, on the eve of his resignation as Prime Minister. At their final audience the Queen offered Churchill a dukedom, which he declined.

INSIGNIA

Order of the Garter
Churchill was invested as a knight companion of the Order by the Queen in April 1953. His installation in the Garter Chapel at Windsor took place in the following year. The Garter was founded by Edward III in 1348 and is the most senior of the English Orders of Chivalry; it is in the sole gift of the Sovereign. Its members consist of the Sovereign, 29 knight companions and members of the royal family and foreign royalties. In accordance with custom, the insignia of the Order were returned to the Queen on Churchill's death and have been graciously lent to Chartwell by Her Majesty. A replica of Churchill's Garter standard hangs from the rafters of the Study.

The insignia of some of the other orders of which Churchill was a member are shown on the shelves below the display cases opposite.

UNIFORMS AND ROBES

FROM LEFT TO RIGHT:

Undress uniform of an Elder Brother of Trinity House
This ancient fraternity obtained its first charter from Henry VIII in 1514. It was primarily to act 'for the relief, increase and augmentation of the Shipping of this realm of England'. Churchill became an Elder Brother in 1913 when First Lord of the Admiralty. The office appealed to his sense of the romantic, and he often wore the impressive full dress uniform (see below) on state occasions.

Service dress of an Air Commodore of the Royal Auxiliary Air Force
The Royal Auxiliary Air Force was founded in 1924. Churchill was appointed Honorary Air Commodore of 615 (County of Surrey) Squadron in April 1939.

Robes of the Chancellor of Bristol University
Churchill became Chancellor of Bristol University in 1929 and held the office until his death. He was also Rector of Aberdeen and Edinburgh universities, and received 21 honorary degrees from universities all over the world.

Full dress of a Privy Councillor, and cocked hat with ostrich plume
The Privy Council has a long history. In the Middle Ages it consisted simply of the sovereign's chief advisers and was often the effective instrument of government. Since the early eighteenth century the

Council has been a largely formal body transacting formal business, though the sovereign refers certain matters to standing committees of the Council (such as the Judicial Committee) or to committees set up for a special purpose. All members of the Cabinet are privy councillors, as are leading figures in the opposition parties, and in recent years there have usually been about 200 councillors. They are entitled to the prefix 'Right Honourable'; other MPs are merely 'Honourable'.

Churchill was appointed in 1907, when he was in office for the first time as Under-Secretary for the Colonies.

Tropical service dress with regimental badges
This uniform was probably first worn by Churchill in Cairo in 1942. The badges are those of the Royal Sussex Regiment.

Full dress of the Lord Warden of the Cinque Ports and a silver-gilt nef presented to Churchill with the Freedom of Hastings in 1947
Churchill was appointed Lord Warden of the Cinque Ports and Constable of Dover Castle in 1941 and was installed by the Grand Court of Shepway in August 1946. He was only the second commoner to hold the office, the first being the Duke of Wellington.

Full dress uniform of an Elder Brother of Trinity House, and a silver demi-lion rampant on a drum plinth
The Lion (the Trinity House crest) was presented to Churchill by the Elder Brethren on his eightieth birthday.

Siren suit, ten-gallon hat and slippers embroidered in gold thread with the initials 'WSC'
Long before the war Churchill wore denim boiler-suits for brick-laying and working at Chartwell. During the war he had them made of light gaberdine as a practical and comfortable mode of attire; he christened them 'Siren Suits'. He also had them made in velvet, chiefly to wear in the evening at home.

The 'ten-gallon' hat was often worn by Churchill when painting in the open in the south of France or at home. At Chartwell the hat was generally adorned with a number of swan or goose feathers picked up during his walks in the garden.

Facsimile Garter robes and bonnet and eighteenth-century star of the Order
The robes and bonnet are lent by Madame Tussaud's. The star is a replica of that which belonged to

Churchill's greatest ancestor, the 1st Duke of Marlborough.

Service dress of a full Colonel in the 4th Queen's Own Hussars
The regiment of dragoons that became the 4th Hussars was raised by James II in 1685 in the aftermath of the Monmouth Rebellion. In its long and distinguished history it won battle honours in the Peninsula, the Crimea, Afghanistan, Flanders, Alamein and Italy. In the 1950s it was amalgamated with the 8th King's Royal Irish Hussars.

On 20 February 1895 Churchill was gazetted a 2nd Lieutenant in the Queen's Own Hussars, and served with the regiment on the North-West Frontier in 1897. He soon left the army to pursue his political ambitions, but in 1941 was made an honorary colonel of the regiment. Curiously, the buttons are those of the Royal Sussex Regiment.

MEDALS

The medals that were presented to Churchill are in the keeping of Winston Churchill, MP, as heirlooms. Those on display were bought by the National Trust in 1966. They include the Queen's Sudan Medal, which was awarded to Churchill following the historic charge of the 21st Lancers at the Battle of Omdurman in 1898, in which he took part.

Wearing the uniform of the 4th Queen's Own Hussars, he received the Médaille Militaire from the French Prime Minister, Paul Ramadier, in Paris in 1947, and the Croix de la Libération, from the hands of De Gaulle in 1958.

THE STUDY

This room was Churchill's workshop for over 40 years. Here he worked on five budgets as Chancellor of the Exchequer from 1924 to 1929, and dictated a stream of memos to his ministerial colleagues on every subject, whether large or small. Out of office in the 1930s, he brought to this room worried political and military advisers to discuss the spread of Fascism in Europe. Here he rehearsed the speeches with which he tried to stir the House of Commons and the Chamberlain government to action. And in this room he conceived his vast literary output. Often late into the night he would stride up and down dictating page after page to a

chain of secretaries. The last volumes of *The World Crisis, Marlborough, The Second World War* and *A History of the English-Speaking Peoples* were all largely written in the Study.

Tilden removed the ceiling to reveal the beams and rafters of the older building that preceded the Victorian house, and inserted the Tudor doorway with its moulded architrave. The windows look west across the front lawn to Crockham Hill and east across the garden to the lakes.

Originally, Churchill slept here in a four-poster bed, but from about the mid-1930s he used the room beyond as his bedroom, which enjoys an unimpeded view of the Weald of Kent.

PICTURES

BETWEEN BOOKSHELVES:

ALFRED JOHNSON, fl.1875–87
Lord Randolph Churchill (1849–95)
Pen and sepia ink.
Lord Randolph is shown in the drawing-room of his London home. The bureau-bookcase is that which now stands against the opposite wall.

OVER DOOR TO STAIRS:

JOHN LEWIS BROWN, 1829–90
Two Cavalry Officers
Signed and dated 1875.
This scene from the Seven Years War was given to Churchill by Sir Philip Sassoon (apparently under the mistaken impression that it showed an episode from his ancestor Marlborough's campaigns), and was afterwards copied by him.

OVER LEFT-HAND DOOR TO BEDROOM:

DUTCH SCHOOL, nineteenth-century
Shipping Scene

Photograph of Queen Elizabeth II taken on her way to open her first Parliament.

EDWIN WARD, fl.1883–c.1927
Lord Randolph Churchill (1849–95) at his desk
Churchill's father is shown working on the budget he was never to deliver during his brief period as Chancellor of the Exchequer from July to December 1886. (A page from his calculations hangs beside the picture.) A brilliant career was predicted for Lord Randolph, but his radical brand of Toryism made him as many enemies as friends in his own party, and after his resignation from the government in 1886, he spent the rest of his short life in the political wilderness. Churchill dedicated his career to restoring Lord Randolph's reputation and achieving what his father had been denied. The black Treasury box which Churchill used when Chancellor (1924–9) sits below.

SARAH CHURCHILL, 1914–82
Winston Churchill, seated, from behind
Pen, ink and pencil.

OVERMANTEL:

ENGLISH SCHOOL, 1770s
Blenheim Palace
The great baroque country home of the Dukes of Marlborough was built by Vanbrugh between 1705 and 1724. This view shows the north front from Rosamund's Well, with, in the foreground, Vanbrugh's monumental bridge and the lake added by 'Capability' Brown in the eighteenth century. Here, on 30 November 1874, Churchill was born, while his parents were staying with his grandfather, the 7th Duke of Marlborough.

RIGHT OF FIREPLACE:

SARAH CHURCHILL, 1914–82
Winston Churchill in profile
Red and black chalk.

Photographs of Franklin Delano Roosevelt and King George VI.

OVER RIGHT-HAND DOOR:

ENGLISH SCHOOL, early nineteenth-century
Portrait of a young girl

JOHN SINGER SARGENT, RA, 1856–1925
Jennie Jerome, Lady Randolph Churchill (1854–1921)

ABOVE LECTERN:

Sir JOHN LAVERY, RA, 1856–1941
Clementine Churchill (1885–1977)
A sketch painted in 1916, while Churchill was serving on the Western Front. Churchill was encouraged in his first efforts at painting by Lavery and his wife, who taught him how to use oils.

SCULPTURE

ON WINDOW SILL BEYOND DESK:
Lady Randolph Churchill's hand
Bronze.

A fragment of shrapnel
During the First World War this 20-pound shell fragment landed between Churchill and his cousin, the 9th Duke of Marlborough. It is inscribed by the Duke 'this fragment fell between us and might have separated us for ever, but is now a token of union.'

ON RIGHT-HAND WINDOW SILL:

HERBERT HASELTINE, 1877–1962
A horse and foal
Bronze.

FURNITURE

The nineteenth-century reproduction mahogany table with claw-and-ball feet by the window was inherited by Churchill from his father. At this table he conceived his biography of Marlborough, his war memoirs and *A History of the English-Speaking Peoples*. On it stand photographs of his family and mementos given him by friends and admirers:

LEFT TO RIGHT:

Photograph of Mary Churchill (Lady Soames).

Photograph after a drawing by Jocelin Bodley of the South African prime minister Jan Smuts.

Churchill's favourite photograph of Lady Churchill, taken when she launched the aircraft-carrier HMS *Indomitable*, in 1940. He later painted a copy of it.

Miniature of Lord Randolph Churchill.

Biscuit-porcelain Sèvres bust of Napoleon, signed by Antoine-Denis Chaudet (1763–1810), and with the initials 'A.B.' for Alexandre Brachard jeune, who worked as a repairer at Sèvres between 1784 and 1827.

A modern silver inkstand, engraved with the Churchill and Spencer crests.

Photograph of Winston Churchill, MP, and his wife on their engagement.

Porcelain bust of Nelson, given to Churchill by Lord Northcliffe.

A small watercolour of a four-in-hand in Jerome Park, New York, with Churchill's maternal grandfather, Leonard Jerome, on the box.

On the blotter are a pair of Churchill's spectacles, a cigar-cutter and a collection of treasury tags.

Propped against a leg of the table is one of Churchill's monthly engagement cards, for July 1937. It was a typically hectic month: he spoke four times in the House of Commons, put the finishing touches to *Great Contemporaries* and was hard at work on the final volume of *Marlborough*.

IN LEFT-HAND BOOKCASE:

A Swiss clock, with a perpetual movement by Jaeger-le-Coultre, driven by changes in atmospheric pressure. Given by the people of Switzerland.

The stuffed toys were gifts from wellwishers.

BEYOND BOOKCASE:

A shield bearing the arms of Malta, given by the people of the island. The defence of Malta against repeated German and Italian bombing was one of the most heroic episodes in the Second World War, for which the island was awarded the George Cross in 1942.

LEFT OF DOOR TO STAIRS:

An aquarium on a seventeenth-century oak chest. In the late 1940s a small boy arrived at the Churchills' London home bearing two black Mollies as a birthday present for Churchill. Sir Winston, deeply touched, bought a tank to hold them, and added to the collection in later years.

RIGHT OF DOOR:

A leather-covered chest bearing the cipher of Queen Anne. Though acquired by Lady Churchill, it is the type of ambassadorial chest that might well have been used by the 1st Duke of Marlborough.

A mahogany card table, on which are dispatch boxes and papers relating to the official history of the Second World War.

AGAINST RIGHT-HAND WALL:

A mahogany lectern, presented to Churchill by his children in 1949. It replaced a simple unvarnished deal desk of similar design made by the local carpenter to Churchill's specifications, which stood in the same position. The books on the lectern include a commemorative volume of the Laying of the Foundation Stone of the rebuilt House of Commons in 1948, minutes about the use of Churchill's telegrams by official historians, and two volumes of Hansard, the official Parliamentary record.

A mahogany bureau-bookcase with Gothic glazing and elaborately crested cornice, which belonged to Lord Randolph Churchill.

FLAGS

OVER FIREPLACE:

The Union Flag, hoisted in Rome on the night of 5 June 1944, was the first British flag to fly over a liberated capital. It was a gift from Field-Marshall Alexander.

A duplicate of Churchill's standard as a Knight of the Garter made at the same time as that which hung in St George's Chapel, Windsor.

Churchill's standard as Lord Warden of the Cinque Ports. This was flown at Chartwell as Churchill's house-flag and a smaller version served as the pennant on his car. Churchill's secretary, Grace Hamblin, reported the arrival of the standard at Chartwell on 23 July 1946. Knowing her fondness for Lewis Carroll's *Through the Looking Glass*, he responded delightedly: 'Oh frabjous day! Callooh! Callay! And then he chortled in his joy.' The memo now hangs in the entrance doorway.

CARPET

A Khorassan, given to Churchill on his 69th birthday by the Shah of Persia during the conference of the Allied Powers held in Teheran in November-December 1943.

THE STAIRS

PICTURES

ON LANDING:

WALTER M. KEESEY, MC, 1887–1970
The First Tank – Somme 1916
Etching, dated 1920.
Churchill was one of the first to grasp the impor-

tance of mechanised armour for modern warfare. Despite the almost universal opposition of the military establishment, he insisted that a prototype 'tank' (its official codename) be built and tested in May 1915. In September 1916 32 tanks saw action for the first time at Le Sars during the Battle of the Somme.

C398 *Island on Lake Geneva from Choisy with Mt Blanc in the Distance*, 1946

C196 *The Valley of the Ourika*, c.1935
The Atlas Mountains appear in the distance. Churchill painted in Morocco over a span of more than twenty years.

C395 *Lake Como*

SCULPTURE

AUGUSTE TREMONT, 1893–
Lion
Given by the people of Luxembourg.

AT FOOT OF STAIRS:

Sir JOHN LAVERY, RA, 1856–1941
Winston Churchill
He is shown in his uniform as colonel of the 6th Battalion, the Royal Scots Fusiliers, which he commanded in Flanders from January to May 1916.

Edward, Duke of Windsor; by Mme Haas (Stairs). Churchill was one of the King's strongest supporters during the Abdication Crisis of 1936

The helmet he wore in action, the characteristically crested model of the French infantry, hangs below the painting, which was presented by the Armoured Car Squadrons.

ON STAIRS TO DINING ROOM:

LEFT WALL:

C473 *Cap d'Ail*, 1952
Churchill painted many of his later pictures at Cap d'Ail when staying with his life-long friend, the newspaper magnate Lord Beaverbrook at his villa, La Capponcina, which is seen in the foreground.

RIGHT WALL:

Sir JOHN LAVERY, RA, 1856–1941
Randolph Churchill (1911–68)
A sketch inscribed: 'To Mrs Churchill from John Lavery 28th May 1932.'

C341 *View through the Arch of the Bridge over the Var, Aix-en-Provence*, c.1930

SCULPTURE

ON SILL:

Mme HAAS
Edward, Duke of Windsor (1894–1972)
Tungum alloy.
Churchill was one of the King's most stalwart supporters during the Abdication Crisis of 1936. Presented to Churchill in 1954.

Modern Capodimonte porcelain group of *Time (?) driving a Chariot*.

MANUSCRIPTS

IN STAIR LOBBY (BEHIND CURTAIN):

Pages from the typescript of the concluding paragraphs of Volume III, Chapter XI, of *The World Crisis*, with Churchill's manuscript corrections.

On the stairs are more cartoons of Churchill and photographs of his horses.

THE DINING ROOM

The Dining Room forms the ground floor of the new wing which Tilden threw out into the garden, but because of the steeply sloping site it is an entire level below the ground floor of the entrance front. The door leads directly out into the garden, which surrounds the room, and windows on three sides

The Dining Room

provide extensive views in all directions. The vivid green glazed chintz curtains add to the garden mood.

Before the Second World War the family took all the main meals of the day here. Round this table Churchill and his political and service colleagues argued out his lonely stand against the appeasement of Hitler in the 1930s. It was also the scene of much conviviality with family and friends. In Churchill's later years the Dining Room was converted into a cinema and a regular Sunday night film-show was held, attended by family, guests and staff. The room has now been returned to its pre-war appearance.

FIREPLACE

The seventeenth-century Sussex fireback depicts St George and a lion rampant.

PICTURES

C177 *Bottlescape*, c.1932
One Christmas Churchill painted a collection of his favourite vintages and one of the Italian dwarf altar candlesticks which have always stood on the side-table below.

C391 *Sketch of Lake Carezza*, Dolomites, 1949

C388 *Fontaine de Vaucluse*, 1948
The fountain is famous for its association with the fourteenth-century Italian poet Petrarch, who had a rural retreat at Vaucluse.

C371 *The Bridge*, south of France, c.1935

C172 *Nasturtiums*, c.1935

WILLIAM NICHOLSON, 1872–1949
Breakfast at Chartwell
It shows the Churchills taking breakfast together (as they rarely did) in this room in the early 1930s. On the table may be seen their much-loved marmalade cat, Tango, and a porcelain rabbit, and, in the right-hand corner, a bantam cock has wandered in from the garden. This is an abandoned first version of the picture commissioned by friends to celebrate the Churchill's silver wedding in 1933. Nicholson borrowed the completed version for a retrospective exhibition of his work at the National Gallery in 1942, took against it, tried, but failed, to improve it, and instead destroyed it – an interesting precedent for Lady Churchill's destruction of Graham Sutherland's portrait of her husband.

BOOK

The Golden Rose Book
This elephant folio bound in vellum was given to the Churchills in 1958 for their golden wedding by

their children. It contains watercolours of 29 of the 32 yellow and gold species, also their children's gift, planted in the walled vegetable garden to commemorate the anniversary. The artists include Augustus John, Duncan Grant, Ivon Hitchens, Matthew Smith and John Nash. The book mark was the gift of Sir George Bellew, Garter King of Arms.

FURNITURE AND FURNISHINGS

The circular dining-tables, side-tables and chairs were commissioned by the Churchills in the 1920s from Heal's, which later marketed the side-table commercially. The tables, of unstained, unvarnished oak, follow a plain seventeenth-century design. The chairs were built to Churchill's detailed specifications (see p.19).

The handsome veneered radiogram was a particular favourite with the Churchill children, who in the 1930s enjoyed dancing to the popular tunes of the

One of Augustus John's illustrations to the Golden Rose Book (Dining Room)

day. Churchill himself was fond of listening to marches and the light operas of Gilbert and Sullivan.

ON TABLE IN CENTRE OF ROOM:

A crystal vase presented to Churchill in 1955, when he received the Freedom of the borough of Harrow. Churchill went to Harrow School and in later years was fond of launching into the school's songs at unexpected moments.

BELOW NICHOLSON PAINTING:

A Copenhagen punch-bowl, given to Churchill by a group of Danish admirers. It is dedicated in Danish to Commodore Olbert Fischer, who commanded the Danish squadron at the Battle of Copenhagen on 2 April 1801. The frieze in grisaille represents incidents in the engagement, in which Nelson, one of Churchill's heroes, played a prominent part. It is one of 25 such bowls made in 1805–7, of which only a dozen have survived.

Nearby is a pile of cigar boxes, which contained his favourite brands of Havanas, Romeo y Julieta and Camacho, the latter especially stamped for Churchill's use. He acquired a taste for good cigars when in Cuba covering the 1895 insurrection as correspondent for the *Daily Graphic*. The cigar subsequently became an inseparable part of Churchill's public image.

ON SIDE-TABLE:

A Japanese lacquer box inlaid with mother-of-pearl. It was a present on Churchill's ninetieth birthday from Shigem Yoshida (Prime Minister of Japan, 1946–7, 1948–54).

Two Italian dwarf altar candlesticks.

CARPETS

The rush matting was specially woven for the room.

THE DINING ROOM PASSAGE

C36 *Tea at Chartwell, c.1928*
Taking tea in the Dining Room on 29 August 1927 are (from left to right) Mrs Thérèse Sickert, Diana Mitford, Edward Marsh, Winston Churchill, Prof. Lindemann, Randolph Churchill, Diana Churchill, Mrs Churchill and W. R. Sickert. Painted from a photograph by Donald Ferguson in the Chartwell visitors' book.

CHAPTER NINE

THE GARDEN

In Chartwell Bulletin No. 12 Churchill wrote to his wife, 'I think it is very important to have animals, flowers and plants in one's life while it lasts'.[1] The Chartwell garden gave him all these in profusion for over 40 years. Here he could relax completely, build a wall, feed a duck or simply enjoy the scent of a magnolia; he could contemplate the past and plan for the future. It was never a grand garden, but is none the worse for that. Clementine liked simple effects and, helped by her expert Head Gardeners, Albert Hill and (after the war) Mr Vincent, she knew how to achieve them with a mass of white geraniums or soft-coloured cherry-pie.

HISTORY

The landscape surrounding Chartwell is ancient, becoming gradually more modern as one approaches the house. Oldest are the gentle hills to west and east, which form a shallow combe, opening at the southern end on to the distant view of the Weald of Kent. Settlers in the thirteenth or fourteenth centuries established the field patterns which can still be seen in the hedgerows and copses that divide the neighbouring farmland. Probably around the same date the hillside beyond the lakes to the east was planted with beeches and oaks. In the eighteenth century the valley bottom became open parkland grazed by sheep, and the hanging woods were renewed. The landscape in its essentials has changed very little since, although in the early nineteenth century what is now the lower lake was created by damming the stream that ran through the valley.

The Victorian owners of Chartwell planted the garden with the ornamental conifers they thought appropriate to their grand new mansion – Wellingtonias, Monkey Puzzle Trees, yews and *Cryp-*

tomerias. Most of the large trees that still decorate the garden date from this period. The Campbell Colquhouns also planted substantial shrubberies around the house and rhododendrons and more conifers on the slopes beyond the Mapleton Road facing the entrance front.

The Churchills removed the overgrown planting around the house, and created almost all the architectural and water features and the herbaceous borders we see in the garden today. However, they did almost nothing to the ancient woodland, for they strove above all to make their new garden complement the superb natural setting which had first drawn Churchill to Chartwell.

At the suggestion of the National Trust, Clementine chose the distinguished American garden designer and writer Lanning Roper to carry on her work when the house was opened by the Trust in 1966. He concentrated principally on developing the planting in the borders along the lines she had laid out, but he was also responsible for new schemes around the car-park, south of the house, and in the Old Kitchen Garden.

On 16 October 1987 Kent suffered what was probably its worst storm in 300 years. It brought down apple trees planted by Churchill in the Orchard and four large trees in the Victorian shrubbery south-west of the Croquet Lawn. But undoubtedly the most catastrophic damage was suffered by the ancient woodland to the north and east, where between 70 and 80 per cent of the trees were lost. The Grove to the south-east was left almost completely naked; much replanting has been done, but it will be many years before it regains its old character.

The upper lake, with Chartwell beyond

THE WATER GARDEN

The visitor enters the garden at its northern end along paths paved since Churchill's time to take the large number of visitors that Chartwell now receives. Ahead is a large clump of dark green *Gunnera manicata*, and a bank of dwarf juniper and cotoneaster. Beyond stands a huge cedar of Lebanon planted by the Campbell Colquhouns and now fully mature. Above the greystone walls of the Rose Garden rises the north front of Chartwell. This was always the least public side of the house, containing the kitchen, office and staff quarters. From the entrance path one can enjoy one's first view of the Chartwell lakes and parkland, which we will explore in more detail later.

The flagged path to the right leads up past a *Magnolia soulangeana* to the Goldfish Pond, one of the most magical parts of the garden. Sadly, the tall trees which once formed the backdrop to this secluded spot were brought down in the Great Storm. However, the shrubs that fringe the shallow pool still stand: bamboos, cotoneaster, acers and *Hydrangea paniculata*. If Churchill's spirit still hovers anywhere in the garden, it is here. For in old age

Churchill loved to sit beside the pool in the simple garden chair, painting, or feeding the fat golden orfe whose descendants still swim in the tranquil waters of this pool.

By the garden wall of Kent ragstone is a border of *Kalmia* 'Clementine Churchill'. Between this wall and a *Cryptomeria japonica* the path takes the visitor to another in the chain of pools that make up the Water Garden. Connecting them are waterfalls and rockwork, brought in at great effort and expense, and laid down to resemble natural outcrops covered in moss and ferns. Behind the pool Clementine planted a bed of white foxgloves and blue anchusa. This was one of the Churchill children's favourite parts of the garden, as the secluded setting made an ideal spot for playing detectives. To one side is the Chart Well which gave its name to the place.

Steps lead to the Entrance Lawn.

THE ENTRANCE LAWN

The Churchills removed the shrubbery which had made Victorian Chartwell so gloomy, and replaced it with a low yew hedge around the new house and an open lawn facing the Mapleton Road. All that remains from the Victorian period are a copper beech and two huge lime trees which are alive with bees when they are in blossom in late June. Churchill built a two-storey tree house for his children 20 feet up one of these limes. When young Sarah Churchill asked her cousin Peregrine why he was subdividing it still further, he replied, 'This is my study, there are times when men have to be alone.'[2]

To shelter the house from the growing volume of traffic on the road, Churchill erected a brick wall, which is now covered in *Clematis montana* and *Pyracantha*. The arrangement of dentils beneath a sloped coping was based on brickwork at Quebec

House in Westerham, the birthplace of General Wolfe and now also the property of the National Trust. Churchill is said to have got the idea from the garden wall at Quebec House, which stands beside the turning to Chartwell.

Despite security considerations Churchill insisted that the large oak entrance gates should remain open. Although he did not mix much in Westerham society, he paid his dues as a local celebrity,

becoming Vice-President of the Westerham town band and cricket club.

By the mid-1930s the Victorian rhododendrons on the hillside beyond the Mapleton Road had become overgrown with unsightly elder and sycamore. Churchill had these removed so that in spring a sheet of uninterrupted colour spreads up from the wood to the trees on the ridge, most of which were carried away in the Great Storm.

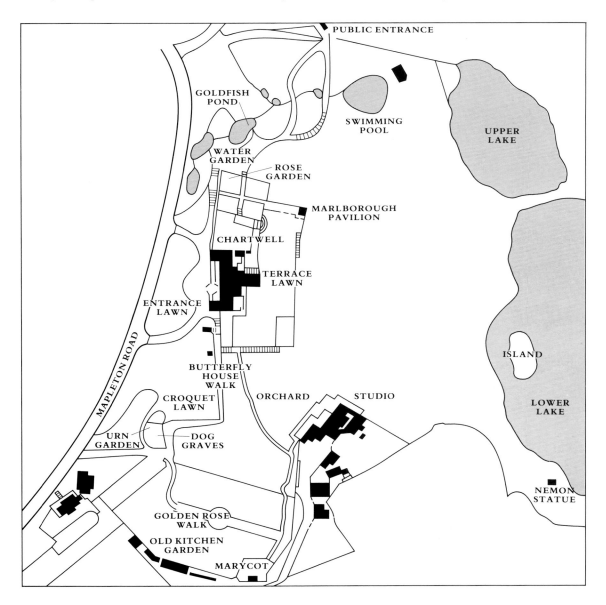

THE ROSE GARDEN

Visitors emerge from the north-east corner of the house on to a small paved terrace. From here one can take in properly the grassy terrace below and the broad park landscape, which has been glimpsed through the windows of the east wing. On the wall to the right of the exit door is a slate tablet commemorating the 17 benefactors who generously donated Chartwell to the National Trust in 1946 on condition that the Churchills could remain living there for the rest of their lives: Lord Camrose, Lord Bearsted, Lord Bicester, Sir James Caird, Sir Hugo Cunliffe-Owen, Lord Catto, Lord Glendyne, Lord Kenilworth, Lord Leathers, Sir James Lithgow, Sir Edward Mountain, Lord Nuffield, Sir Edward Peacock, Lord Portal, J. Arthur Rank, James de Rothschild and Sir Frederick Stewart.

Beyond the small lawn to the north of the house is the walled Rose Garden laid out by Clementine with the advice of her cousin Venetia Montagu. Paths divide it into four with beds of hybrid tea

Rose 'Etude' in the Chartwell garden

roses. (When Clementine planned the garden in the 1920s, the fashion for floribundas and the revival of old-fashioned roses were scarcely underway.) Four standard wisterias grow where the paths meet, and the mixed borders beneath the surrounding walls are filled with soft-coloured plants, including cherry-pie, penstemons, catmint and fuchsias.

THE MARLBOROUGH PAVILION

The right-hand path leads out of the Rose Garden under a vine-covered pergola to the Marlborough Pavilion. This was built as a summer-house by Tilden in the mid-1920s, and decorated in 1949 by Churchill's nephew, the interior designer John Spencer Churchill. The theme of the decoration is Churchill's greatest ancestor, John Churchill, 1st Duke of Marlborough. On the north wall are the 1st Duke's coat of arms and the family's Spanish motto, *Fiel Pero Desdichado* ('Faithful but Unfortunate') – a reference to the loyalty of the 1st Duke's father to the Royalist cause after the execution of Charles I in 1649. Four terracotta plaques on the walls represent rivers that played a part in Marlborough's campaigns during the War of the Spanish Succession (1702–13): the Danube, the Rhine (with the sirens of the Lorelei), the Meuse and the Moselle. The terracotta medallions at the corners represent the 1st Duke; his wife Sarah; Queen Anne; and Prince Eugene of Savoy, Marlborough's most steadfast Continental ally, who played an important part in the victories of Blenheim (1704), Oudenarde (1708) and Malplaquet (1709). The low-relief frieze around the ceiling evokes the Marlborough wars. One panel shows the defence of the village of Blenheim, the climactic moment of the 1st Duke's most famous victory.

THE TERRACE LAWN

From the Marlborough Pavilion a broad terraced lawn stretches south around the east front of the house. On a hot day the old yew planted by the Campbell Colquhouns offers welcome shade. From

A vine-covered pergola leads from the Rose Garden to the Marlborough Pavilion

the lawn one can enjoy the superb view south out over the Weald of Kent, and also appreciate the projecting east wing which was Tilden's principal addition to the house. *Hydrangea petiolaris* covers part of this wing, and a wisteria almost smothers the adjoining staircase block, which is surmounted by a little cupola and ship weathervane – again Tilden additions. From the far end of the lawn, where a huge chestnut has happily survived the Great Storm, the south front of the house is visible. Clementine planted a *Magnolia grandiflora*, which has reached a substantial height, against the trellis-work attached to this front. Churchill could enjoy the lemon scent of its waxy white flowers from the bay window of his bedroom on the first floor.

THE BUTTERFLY HOUSE WALK

Take the steps up from the south-west corner of the Terrace Lawn to the straight path which is lined on the right by a high yew hedge and drops away on the left to the Orchard. Clementine planted the borders here with buddleias to encourage the butterflies which Churchill loved to see in the garden. Worried by the decline in Britain's native species, Churchill called in a butterfly breeding expert after the war for advice on converting the little summer-house at the end of this walk to incubate butterfly larvae. He took a childlike delight in watching the young butterflies emerge and opening the door of his butterfly house to give them their freedom. In a moment of cheerful fantasy he even proposed erecting 'fountains of honey and water' in the Rose Garden where they

(Above) The colourful
border above the Old
Kitchen Garden

(Right) One of
Churchill's walls in the
Old Kitchen Garden

Churchill at work on one of his walls; his daughter Sarah acts as bricklayer's mate

might feed.[3] The National Trust continues to encourage butterflies (along more practical lines), so that peacocks, tortoiseshells, brimstones and commas, and later in the summer red admirals and painted ladies, are all a common sight in the garden. Lanning Roper introduced the silver-foliage plants here, including *Brachyglottis* 'Sunshine' and Cotton Lavender.

THE CROQUET LAWN

The path and yew hedge turn sharply to the right to reveal the Croquet Lawn. Before the Churchills came to Chartwell, this area was a vegetable garden. Clementine had it levelled and transformed into a tennis court, as she was a very keen and accomplished player in the 1930s. After the war it became a croquet lawn where Clementine enjoyed a game with family and friends. Churchill was only an occasional player. When he could be persuaded to compete, he wielded the croquet mallet single-handed like the polo stick with which he had become expert as a young man.

Beyond the Croquet Lawn two flagstones are set into the path marking the graves of Churchill's brown poodles, Rufus I and Rufus II, to whom he was devoted. His cat Jock I, who died in 1974, is similarly commemorated nearby.

THE OLD KITCHEN GARDEN

The high brick wall ahead encloses what was formerly the kitchen garden, which supplied Chartwell and, in the war years, No. 10, with a reliable supply of fresh vegetables. After the National Trust took over in 1965, it was mostly laid down to grass.

The path straight ahead leads to a further small terrace lawn with seats looking over the Weald. During the 1920s and '30s this sunny spot was occupied by greenhouses and potting sheds; after the war Clementine's first project in the garden was to sweep away what had become antiquated buildings and create an open terrace in their place. She also designed the arch-backed garden seats here.

Beyond the wall to the right are two houses. One was an old building, enlarged and improved by Churchill when he took on Chartwell. From the time of the Campbell Colquhouns, it was the home of the Head Gardener, and it is still lived in by one of the Chartwell gardeners. The second was built by Churchill in the 1920s. It was let for a time to a relative, Horatia Seymour, and was then used by the butler. It is now the Administrator's house.

The terrace is a good place from which to enjoy the Golden Rose Walk in the centre of the garden below. It was created in 1958 as a golden wedding present to the Churchills from their children. The walk, which is now paved, contains yellow- and gold-flowering roses planted in two parallel borders flanked by beech hedges. At the centre of the circular feature midway along the walk is a sundial. The plinth is inscribed 'HERE LIES THE BALI DOVE', and round it are lines from a poem by W. P. Ker, suggested to Clementine by Freya Stark:

> It does not do to wander
> Too far from sober men,
> But there's an island yonder,
> I think of it again.

In 1936 Clementine had visited Bali, which she thought an 'enchanted island', while cruising in the South Pacific on Lord Moyne's yacht, the *Rosaura*. A Bali dove, a pinky-beige bird with coral-coloured beak and feet, was brought back in a wicker cage and lived on for several years as a much cherished pet.

A tablet set into the east wall at the bottom end of this garden records that 'the greater part of this wall was built between the years 1925 and 1932 by Winston with his own hands'. The good state of these thick walls is a tribute to Churchill's skill in bricklaying, which was one of his favourite occupations in the inter-war years. He also built the little brick summer-house nearby for his youngest child, Mary; it was christened the 'Marycot' after her.

The plots in the north-east corner of the garden still provide the cut flowers which have always been such an important element in the decoration of Chartwell.

THE ORCHARD

At the bottom end of the Old Kitchen Garden is an archway flanked by Solomon's seal and hostas, which leads into the Orchard. As soon as Churchill took over Chartwell, he began ordering new stock of apple and pear trees to plant here. Many have now reached the end of their natural life or were destroyed in the Great Storm, but replacements of the same old varieties have been planted by the Trust, together with 'Winston' apples.

The oak bench was presented to Churchill on his eightieth birthday by the Epping Conservative Association. He represented the constituency, firstly as Epping, then as Wanstead and Woodford, for almost 40 years.

On the right is a row of tile-hung cottages, whose mellow roofs add so much to the view from the Terrace Lawn. Clementine used to refer to them as her 'village'. Orchard Cottage was extended by Churchill in the local vernacular style in the late 1930s, and used by him on his occasional visits to Chartwell during the Second World War.

THE STUDIO

From 1915 painting was Churchill's principal relaxation from the stresses and strains of politics. His painting life is described by Lady Soames in Chapter Seven. The Studio was built in the 1930s and became a favourite refuge in those years. He loved to work here, when he was not painting out of doors in front of his subject. The walls are hung with many of his unframed canvases in various stages of completion.

PICTURES

ENGLISH, nineteenth-century
Lord Randolph Churchill (1849–95)
In *The Dream* Churchill has described how, when he was copying this damaged portrait, his father appeared before him sitting in the old leather armchair nearby, and how they fell to a long discussion of world events since Lord Randolph's death over 50 years before.

T. LELKOV
'*The Big Three*'
Churchill, Roosevelt and Stalin at the Yalta conference in 1945. Presented to Lady Churchill during her visit to the Soviet Union in 1945. Copied from an illustration in *Trud* of 13 February 1945.

SCULPTURE

ON STAND:

WINSTON CHURCHILL, 1874–1965

C496 *Oscar Nemon* (1906–85)
Churchill's only attempt at sculpture was executed while he was himself being sculpted by Nemon in 1954. It is said to be a remarkable likeness.

(Above) The Studio

(Left) Lord Randolph Churchill; by an unknown artist (Studio). When Churchill was copying this portrait, his father appeared to speak to him

Rudyard Kipling (1865–1936)
Given to Churchill on his eightieth birthday. Inscribed: 'One sang of Empire and the other saved it.'

Lady Randolph Churchill (1854–1921)
Marble.

FURNISHINGS

IN INNER STUDIO:

Churchill's easel, with an unfinished canvas upon it, stands at the centre of the large recess. Near at hand is a generous supply of oil paints in capacious tubes. The armchair in which he painted was given him by his friend Sir Ian Hamilton.

OVER STUDIO DOOR:

Stuffed head of a bull killed by the great Spanish matador Manolete at Valencia on VE Day, 8 May 1945.

The large modern tapestry once hung in the Belgium Parliament. Churchill admired it when he went to Brussels to receive the Freedom of the city, and it was afterwards given to him.

UNDER WINDOW:

The huge globe, one of two made specially for Churchill and Roosevelt, was the gift of the United States War Department.

ON OAK TABLE:

Model of a naval gun made and presented in 1918 by workers in the Ponders End Shell Works in London.

BESIDE TABLE:

A bundle of Churchill's polo sticks and a further selection of walking sticks given to him over the years.

ON TABLE TO RIGHT:

Mementos of the Second World War, including Churchill's wartime passport, ration book and identity card.

THE LAKES

The open parkland that sweeps down from the Orchard and the Terrace Lawn to the lakes and up to the woodland beyond, dates back to the eighteenth century. Churchill removed the bumps and hollows to create the smooth expanse of grass we see today. Much of his spare time at Chartwell was spent enlarging the lower lake, creating a wooded island facing its western bank, and digging out a new lake to the north. The lakes soon became home to a varied assortment of birds on which Churchill doted, as Lady Diana Cooper has described:

'Feeding the poor little birds' is a huge joy to him. They consist of five foolish geese, five furious black swans, two muddy sheldrakes, two white swans – Mr Juno and Mrs Jupiter, so called because they got the sexes wrong to begin with, two Canadian geese ('Lord and Lady Beaverbrook') and some miscellaneous ducks. The basket of bread on Winston's arm is used first to lure and coax and then as ammunition. The great aim is to get them all fighting. 'We must make a policy,' he says; 'you stone them and we will get the five flying fools on their right flank.'[4]

There are still black swans at Chartwell, but to protect them from the local foxes, the northern lake has had to be fenced.

At the south end of the big lake is an over life-size statue of Winston and Clementine Churchill by Oscar Nemon. There is already one cast of the group in Kansas City, but it was Nemon's wish to see a second in Britain. Funds for this cast were raised by the Churchill Statue Trust to mark the fiftieth anniversary of Churchill's appointment as Prime Minister in 1940. It was unveiled in November 1990 by HM Queen Elizabeth the Queen Mother.

THE SWIMMING POOL

Walking back up from the lakes towards the car-park, visitors will see ahead of them the swimming pool. In the early years the Churchills used the lakes for swimming. In the 1930s Churchill built this oval concrete pool, complete with concealed underground boilers to heat the water to 75°F. With his usual thoroughness he took advice from his scientist friend, Professor Lindemann, on the amount of water needed to fill it, and from a chemist on the correct chemicals to keep it clean.

NOTES

1 WSC/CC, 13 April 1935. Spencer-Churchill papers. Quoted Gilbert, *Companion*, V, ii, 1981, p.1137.

2 *Thread in the Tapestry*, 1969, p.42.

3 Newman, 1987, p.203.

4 Cooper, 1959, pp.155–6.

FAMILY TREE OF WINSTON AND CLEMENTINE CHURCHILL

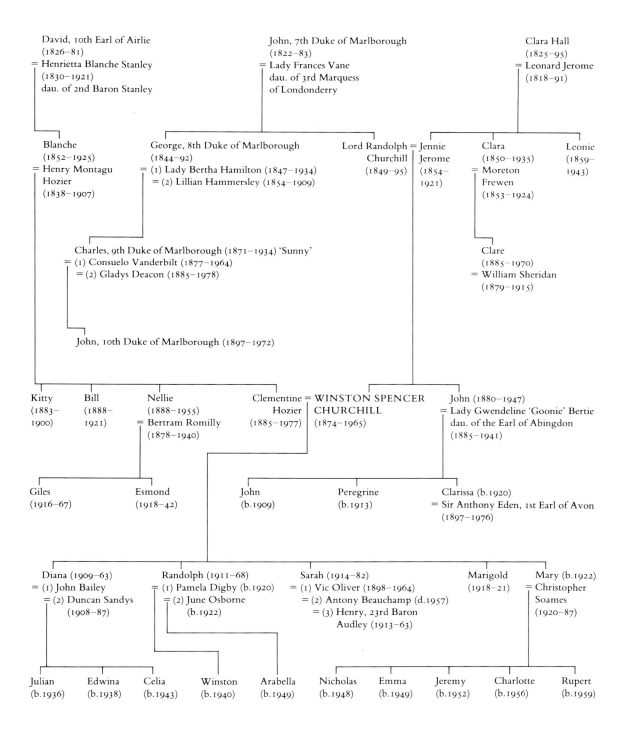

David, 10th Earl of Airlie
(1826–81)
= Henrietta Blanche Stanley
(1830–1921)
dau. of 2nd Baron Stanley

John, 7th Duke of Marlborough
(1822–83)
= Lady Frances Vane
dau. of 3rd Marquess
of Londonderry

Clara Hall
(1825–95)
= Leonard Jerome
(1818–91)

Blanche
(1852–1925)
= Henry Montagu
Hozier
(1838–1907)

George, 8th Duke of Marlborough
(1844–92)
= (1) Lady Bertha Hamilton (1847–1934)
= (2) Lillian Hammersley (1854–1909)

Lord Randolph
Churchill
(1849–95)

= Jennie
Jerome
(1854–
1921)

Clara
(1850–1935)
= Moreton
Frewen
(1853–1924)

Leonie
(1859–
1943)

Charles, 9th Duke of Marlborough (1871–1934) 'Sunny'
= (1) Consuelo Vanderbilt (1877–1964)
= (2) Gladys Deacon (1885–1978)

Clare
(1885–1970)
= William Sheridan
(1879–1915)

John, 10th Duke of Marlborough (1897–1972)

Kitty
(1883–
1900)

Bill
(1888–
1921)

Nellie
(1888–1955)
= Bertram Romilly
(1878–1940)

Clementine
Hozier
(1885–1977)

= WINSTON SPENCER
CHURCHILL
(1874–1965)

John (1880–1947)
= Lady Gwendeline 'Goonie' Bertie
dau. of the Earl of Abingdon
(1885–1941)

Giles
(1916–67)

Esmond
(1918–42)

John
(b.1909)

Peregrine
(b.1913)

Clarissa (b.1920)
= Sir Anthony Eden, 1st Earl of Avon
(1897–1976)

Diana (1909–63)
= (1) John Bailey
= (2) Duncan Sandys
(1908–87)

Randolph (1911–68)
= (1) Pamela Digby (b.1920)
= (2) June Osborne
(b.1922)

Sarah (1914–82)
= (1) Vic Oliver (1898–1964)
= (2) Antony Beauchamp (d.1957)
= (3) Henry, 23rd Baron
Audley (1913–63)

Marigold
(1918–21)

Mary (b.1922)
= Christopher
Soames
(1920–87)

Julian
(b.1936)

Edwina
(b.1938)

Celia
(b.1943)

Winston
(b.1940)

Arabella
(b.1949)

Nicholas
(b.1948)

Emma
(b.1949)

Jeremy
(b.1952)

Charlotte
(b.1956)

Rupert
(b.1959)

BIBLIOGRAPHY

The Churchill papers, deposited in Churchill College, Cambridge, contain extensive correspondence relating to Tilden's rebuilding of Chartwell in 1922–4, and to the running of the Chartwell estate thereafter. The chapter on the garden is indebted to John Meehan's 1988 report on the historical development of the Chartwell landscape.

ASHLEY, Maurice, *Churchill as Historian*, Secker & Warburg, 1968.

BETTLEY, James, *Lush and Luxurious: The life and work of Philip Tilden*, RIBA, 1987.

BIRKENHEAD, The Earl of, *The Prof in Two Worlds*, Collins, 1961.

BRENDON, Piers, *Winston Churchill: A Brief Life*, Secker & Warburg, 1984.

CHURCHILL, John Spencer, *Crowded Canvas*, Odhams, 1961.

CHURCHILL, Randolph S., *Winston S. Churchill. I. Youth, 1874–1900*, Heinemann, 1966; *II. Young Statesman, 1900–1914*, 1967.

CHURCHILL, Sarah, *A Thread in the Tapestry*, André Deutsch, 1967.

CHURCHILL, Winston S., *My Early Life*, Thornton Butterworth, 1930.

CHURCHILL, Winston S., *Painting as a Pastime*, Odhams, 1948.

CHURCHILL, Winston S., *The Second World War*, 6 vols., Cassell, 1948–54.

COLVILLE, John, *The Fringes of Power: Downing Street Diaries 1939–1955*, Hodder & Stoughton, 1985.

COOMBS, David, *Churchill: His Paintings*, Hamish Hamilton, 1967.

COOPER, Diana, *The Light of Common Day*, Hart-Davis, 1959.

EADE, Charles, ed., *Churchill by his Contemporaries*, Hutchinson, 1953.

FEDDEN, Robin, *Churchill and Chartwell*, National Trust, 1968.

GILBERT, Martin, *Winston S. Churchill. III. 1914–1916*, Heinemann, 1971; *IV. 1917–1922*, 1975; *V. 1922–1939*, 1976; *VI. Finest Hour, 1939–1941*, 1983; *VII. Road to Victory, 1941–1945*, 1986; *VIII. Never Despair, 1945–1965*, 1988; and five Companion vols. of documents in 13 parts.

GILBERT, Martin, *Churchill: A Life*, Heinemann, 1991.

HASTED, Edward, *The History and Topographical Survey of the County of Kent*, 1797.

MACMILLAN, Harold, *Winds of Change, 1914–1939*, Macmillan, 1966.

MACMILLAN, Harold, *Tides of Fortune, 1945–1955*, Macmillan, 1969.

NEWMAN, L. Hugh, 'Wings for Winston Churchill', *Country Life*, clxxxi, 3 December 1987, pp.202–3.

PELLING, Henry, *Winston Churchill*, Macmillan, 1974.

RHODES JAMES, Robert, *Lord Randolph Churchill*, Weidenfeld & Nicolson, 1959.

RHODES JAMES, Robert, *Churchill: A Study of Failure 1900–1939*, Weidenfeld & Nicolson, 1970.

SOAMES, Mary, *Clementine Churchill*, Cassell, 1979.

SOAMES, Mary, *Family Album*, Houghton Mifflin, 1982.

SOAMES, Mary, *Winston Churchill: His Life as a Painter*, Collins, 1990.

TILDEN, Philip, *True Remembrances: The Memoirs of an Architect*, Country Life, 1954.

TREE, Ronald, *When the Moon was High*, Macmillan, 1975.

WHEELER-BENNETT, Sir John, ed., *Action This Day: Working with Churchill*, Macmillan, 1968.

INDEX